JOHN A. WIDTSOE

John A. Widtsoe

JOHN A. WIDTSOE

SCIENTIST AND THEOLOGIAN

1872–1952

THOMAS G. ALEXANDER

SIGNATURE BOOKS | 2023 | SALT LAKE CITY

For our children:
Brooke, Brenda, Tracy, Mark, and Paul

Join our mail list at www.signaturebooks.com for details on events and related titles we think you'll enjoy.

Design by Jason Francis

FIRST EDITION | 2023

LIBRARY OF CONGRESS CONTROL NUMBER: 2023945482

Paperback ISBN: 978-1-56085-469-2
Ebook ISBN: 978-1-56085-486-9

CONTENTS

INTRODUCTION

Born in 1872 under adverse circumstances on the Norwegian island of Frøyen, John Andreas Widtsoe survived to become an influential authority on irrigation and dry farming, leader in higher education, and one of the fifteen highest authorities in the Church of Jesus Christ of Latter-day Saints. Widtsoe's father, John Anderson Widtsoe, died while he was yet a child, but his mother, Anna Karine Gaarden Widtsoe, sustained her family as a skilled seamstress. After joining the Latter-day Saints, Anna took her two boys, John, and his brother, Aasbjorn (later anglicized as Osborne) Johannes Peder Widtsoe, to Logan, Utah, where they each worked to sustain themselves as immigrant Saints.

After receiving his earliest education in Norway, John attended schools in Utah. Later, after borrowing money from friends and a bank, Widtsoe received his bachelor's and master's degrees at Harvard University. With a master's degree, he joined Logan's Agricultural College (AC) of Utah's chemistry faculty and served as chemist at the Agricultural Experiment Station.

John fell in love with and married Leah Eudora Dunford. Leaving Logan, John and Leah traveled with their daughter, Anna, and Leah's sister, Emma Lucy Gates, to Germany where he enrolled in chemistry at the University of Göttingen. There Widtsoe studied with Bernhard Tollens, the world's authority on the structures of sugars, starches, and nitrogenous substances. Widtsoe graduated *magna cum laude* with a PhD from Göttingen in 1999. Afterward, he extended his education and contributed to biochemistry in Berlin and Zürich.

In 1900 Widtsoe assumed the directorship of Utah State Agricultural College's Experiment Station. In collaboration with agricultural engineer Lewis A. Merrill, Widtsoe revolutionized the field of dry farming, publishing the standard texts on the subject and influencing the field worldwide. He also conducted research on irrigation farming, producing books and articles as well that influenced the practices of farmers throughout the world.

While Widtsoe directed the experiment station, AC president William J. Kerr sought to reform the curriculum to compete with the University of Utah, ninety miles to the south in Salt Lake City. Widtsoe privately opposed Kerr's program, and Kerr fired him. Widtsoe moved to Brigham Young University in Provo, Utah, where he inaugurated the department of agriculture.

Kerr's efforts to compete with the University of Utah led to his dismissal and to Widtsoe's appointment as USAC president. In his presidency, Widtsoe mended the agricultural college's relationship with the legislature and emphasized farming, mechanic arts, home economics, and commerce as required by the Morrill Act that had established such colleges. He also mended fences with the University of Utah's leaders, which allowed him to introduce agricultural engineering into the USAC curriculum. In the meantime, Leah lobbied with Senator (and LDS apostle) Reed Smoot to secure federal funding for home economics education, which the Widtsoes introduced into the USAC's curriculum.

In 1916, Widtsoe's career again underwent a change as a result of a conflict between University of Utah president Joseph T. Kingsbury and the faculty. The U's board of trustees appointed Widtsoe as president. At Utah Widtsoe endeared himself to the faculty and the alumni by introducing a constitution that gave the faculty a significant role in university administration. He also saved the U's medical school's accreditation while weathering vicissitudes associated with presiding over a university and helping the community cope with shortages during World War I.

In 1921, Widtsoe's life changed again as Heber J. Grant, president of the LDS Church, called him to join the Quorum of the Twelve Apostles. Since his conversion and baptism, Widtsoe had been an active church member. He had contributed to the church in numerous positions in wards and stakes in addition to serving on general boards and writing articles in the *Improvement Era* and books such as *Joseph Smith as Scientist*, which the church used as part of its auxiliaries curriculum. As an apostle working full time, Widtsoe accepted a salary that was a third of what he had earned as University of Utah president. He did so because of his faith and his commitment to the church.

In addition to regular duties such as visiting stake conferences and speaking in church meetings and conferences, Widtsoe assumed the position of commissioner of church education from 1921 to 1924 and again from 1934 to 1936. In this capacity, he worked first with Adam S. Bennion, who served as superintendent of church education from 1919 to 1928. Before Widtsoe assumed the commissionership in 1934, the two positions had been combined. During Widtsoe and Bennion's tenure, the church began reducing its financing of secondary and higher education, and instead began building seminaries to provide religious studies for high school age students and replacing most church colleges with institutes of religion near colleges and universities. In the United States this retrenchment led eventually to the retention of Brigham Young University and Ricks College (now BYU–Idaho) and after 1950 to the construction of the Church College of Hawaii (now BYU–Hawai'i). In 1934 Widtsoe also introduced summer sessions at BYU for church education teachers.

As an apostle, Widtsoe was once again drawn back to Europe. In part because of anti-Mormon propaganda and violence following World War I, many European countries were reluctant to allow Latter-day Saint missionaries to enter their countries to proselytize. On assignment from the First Presidency, Widtsoe worked with governments and with Senator and Apostle Reed Smoot to induce European countries to allow missionaries to reenter and to counter anti-Mormon activity.

From 1927 to 1933, Widtsoe served as the church's European Mission president. In this capacity, he reformed the European mission system by separating the mission president's office from that of the British Mission, moving the European Mission office from Liverpool to London, and calling local Europeans, to the degree they were available, to local leadership positions instead of relying almost entirely on American missionaries. (Of necessity, European Mission president George F. Richards had done the same thing during

World War I.) In addition, Widtsoe opened a mission in Czecho-slovakia and traveled to Palestine, Syria, and Lebanon to dedicate a grave and meet with local leaders.

Both state and federal governments occasionally called on Widt-soe's expertise in irrigation while he served as an apostle. Throughout his apostolic career, Widtsoe served on a number of state boards that addressed irrigation. In September 1922, he participated in a float trip from Hall's Crossing to Lee's Ferry (southern Utah/northern Arizona) to locate potential dam sites for the upper basin states of Wyoming, Colorado, Utah, and New Mexico. Later, in the fall of 1922, Widtsoe served as a consultant to the Colorado River Com-pact Commission and succeeded in convincing the commission to include some of his ideas in the interstate compact.

In 1923–24 Widtsoe served on the Fact Finding Commission established by Congress to identify and propose solutions to the problems on federal reclamation projects established under the Newlands Act. This act led many farmers to become unable to repay the projects' construction and maintenance costs. Unlike many com-mission members, Widtsoe, along with Thomas Campbell, Elwood Mead, and James R. Garfield, attended nearly all of the committee's sessions, and Widtsoe and Campbell drafted virtually all of the fact finders' final report.

Widtsoe was one of three PhD scientists called to the Quorum of the Twelve Apostles during the early twentieth century. In 1911, James E. Talmage, who earned a PhD for non-resident work in 1896 from Illinois Wesleyan University, was called to the apostleship. Widtsoe was called in 1921. In 1899, Joseph F. Merrill earned a PhD from John's Hopkins and was called as an apostle in 1931. All three men worked to reconcile and introduce the truths they had learned in their scientific studies with the teachings of the LDS Church.

Widtsoe's major contributions to the church appeared principally during his co-editorship of the *Improvement Era* with church pres-ident Grant. Widtsoe was called to the co-editorship in 1935. He published a series of articles under the title "Evidences and Recon-ciliations." These were later combined into three books, two with the title of his essays and the third titled *Gospel Interpretations*.

Widtsoe's goal was to publish essays that contained truth as he understood it no matter the source, but especially from science and theology. As a scientist, Widtsoe had learned of the latest advances from the 1930s through the late 1940s. As a theologian, he was intimately familiar with the church's scriptures, and had also studied the sermons on church doctrine and practice by prominent church leaders. He drew on both science and theology for his essays.

Widtsoe's essays considered a large number of topics. Among the most important were: the question of God's existence, relying on theories as a gateway to truth, the extent to which species changed through evolution and how evolution worked, advanced education need not undermine faith, the fallacy of predicting future events such as the time of Christ's return, the beliefs of the world's religions, the problems of Old Testament stories such as Noah's flood and stopping the earth from rotating, the Holy Spirit and the Holy Ghost, the equality of men and women, heaven in the hereafter, priesthood, and, one of his favorites, the Word of Wisdom health code.

Throughout his career as a scientist, educator, university president, and apostle, Widtsoe contributed to a wide range of fields locally, nationally, and internationally. He pushed the boundaries of knowledge on irrigation and dry farming. The only person to have helmed both what became Utah State University and was then the University of Utah, he revolutionized both institutions in part by promoting the advancement of science and by ceding much governing authority to faculties. As an apostle, he reformed the administration of the European Mission and integrated his knowledge of science and scripture to write near-authoritative treatments of church doctrine and of the relation between scientific truth and church theology. The scientific, educational, and Latter-day Saint communities would have been much poorer without Widtsoe's important contributions.

CHAPTER ONE

FROM FRØYEN TO LOGAN

Rimming Norway's thousands of western fjords lies a series of rocky islands surrounded by irregular deep channels. During John A. Widtsoe's childhood, most of the people who inhabited these islands earned their livelihood from fishing. Fishers sailed out into the waters of the North Atlantic either to the Norwegian Sea to the north or to the North Sea to the south to fish for whitefish, salmon, flounder, herring, and especially halibut.[1]

On the island of Frøyen located near the conjunction of Trondheim Fjord and the Atlantic Ocean lived the family of John Andersen Widtsoe and Anna Karine Gaarden Widtsoe. The Widtsoe family owned a two-story home in the village of Daløe. And in that home on January 31, 1872, John's and Anna's first son, John Andreas, was born.[2]

At John Andreas's birth, his parents and the midwife who assisted Anna in his delivery feared he might not live. Their son's wrist was firmly attached to his head. No doctor practiced on Frøyen at the time, so someone present performed a crude operation to separate John's hand from his head. Scars from the surgery marred Widtsoe's head throughout the remainder of his life.[3]

As faithful Lutherans, John and Anna feared that their first son would die. In a desperate effort to "save his son's soul from misery in hell, ... [father Widtsoe and some friends courageously] rowed

---

1. John A. Widtsoe, *In the Gospel Net: The Story of Anna Karine Gaarden Widtsoe* (6th ed.; Salt Lake City: Stevens & Wallis, n.d.), 13, 21–22, 32.

2. Widtsoe, *Gospel Net*, 54–55.

3. John A. Widtsoe, *In a Sunlit Land: The Autobiography of John A. Widtsoe* (Salt Lake City: Milton R. Hunter and G. Homer Durham, 1952), 2.

across the angry [Trondheim] fjord in midwinter, [and] brought back an equally courageous priest," who baptized John by sprinkling.[4]

John Andreas's mother and father came from distinctly different backgrounds. Born in 1849 and raised in the village of Titran on Frøya, one of a series of small villages along the island's Atlantic shore, Anna Gaarden was the oldest daughter of Peder Olsen Gaarden, a "King's Pilot." Peder knew the channels, reefs, and headlands so clearly that he could steer boats around these treacherous hazards with patient confidence.[5] Anna's mother, Beret Martha Haavig, came from Frøya's landed gentry. Beret's father, Jørgen Arnsten Haavig, reportedly a capable businessman, owned the village of Horvik on Frøya. Endowed with the gift of leadership, Jørgen passed the same quality to mother Beret.[6]

John Andreas's father, John Andersen Widtsoe, was born in Øien, a town about forty-five miles south of Trondheim. After John Andersen's birth, the family moved to Trondheim where his father, Anders Johnsen Widtsoe, an apprentice carpenter, constructed the family house.[7]

Unfortunately, John Andersen's mother died when he was only eleven. After his first wife's death, Anders married a second time. Inauspiciously, John Andersen and his stepmother did not get along, and he left home frequently, spending many of his teenage years away, often living with relatives.[8]

Although Anders worried about the future prospects of a son he thought wayward, he came to realize that John Andersen was intelligent after he earned first place in his Lutheran confirmation class. Although John Andersen frequently mucked out local stables to help support himself, his father did not lose faith in his son. Hoping to secure his son's future, Anders met with some local leaders who also recognized John's ability. They encouraged John to become a teacher, and agreed to pay for his education if he promised to return

---

4. Widtsoe, *Sunlit Land*, 2.
5. Widtsoe, *Gospel Net*, 18.
6. Widtsoe, *Gospel Net*, 26.
7. Widtsoe, *Gospel Net*, 43.
8. Widtsoe, *Gospel Net*, 44–45.

to Frøya to teach school. John accepted the challenge, and enrolled in a *seminarium* near Klaebo.[9]

Keeping his promise, at age twenty-one after studying for two years at the *seminarium*, he returned to Frøya. He moved from town to town teaching the island's children. In many of Norway's towns, the local priest, usually the most educated man in the community, assisted parishioners in preparing wills and deeds and writing letters. Since no priest lived on Frøya, John served the role of educated benefactor. Moreover, in addition to writing for his neighbors, as a clergymen might have done in other communities, he visited and comforted the sick, older people, and young children.[10]

In John Andersen's first class, Anna Gaarden, then about twelve, was one of the students. The two became attracted to each other, and eight years after he had begun teaching, they became engaged.[11] Recognizing that although his two years of study qualified him to teach school, John needed two more years of study to graduate from the *seminarium*. With Anna's encouragement, John returned to school where he graduated with high honors.[12] After he returned to Frøya with his degree, on December 29, 1870, John and Anna married. Anna, twenty-one at the time of her marriage, was nine years younger than John.[13] After they married, John resumed his studies, receiving a degree from the University at Oslo.[14]

After teaching a time in Frøya, John decided to discontinue his peripatetic teaching and build a house for his family large enough in which to hold classes. As planned, he built the house in Daløe in which John Andreas was born. The house served both as a home for the family and as a site of classrooms in which students from miles around traveled to study.[15]

In about 1874, John Andersen accepted a teaching position in Namsos, a town about 80 miles north of Trondheim. In addition to

9. Widtsoe, *Gospel Net*, 48–49; Alan K. Parrish, *John A. Widtsoe: A Biography* (Salt Lake City: Deseret Book Co., 2003), 13–14.

10. Widtsoe, *Gospel Net*, 48–49; Parrish, *John A. Widtsoe*, 13–14.

11. Widtsoe, *Gospel Net*, 48–49.

12. Widtsoe, *Gospel Net*, 49–50.

13. Widtsoe, *Gospel Net*, 51.

14. Widtsoe, *Gospel Net*, 54.

15. Widtsoe, *Gospel Net*, 51.

teaching in a graded school that was quite unlike the mixed grades of students he taught in his home in Daløe, John published articles in the local newspaper and served his church as a song leader. A second son, Aasbjorn (later anglicized as Osborne) Johannes Peder Widtsoe, was born on December 12, 1877.[16]

Unfortunately, in February 1878, when Osborne was only two months old and John Andreas was only seven, John Andersen fell ill while teaching. As he suffered in severe pain, John learned he had a telescoped intestine. Unfortunately, medical knowledge had not advanced sufficiently at the time or a surgeon might have performed surgery on his bowels. Instead, in excruciating pain, John Andersen died at home.[17]

John Andersen was only thirty-eight at the time of his death, and although his young widow taught school in Namsos for a while, she preferred to live elsewhere. She moved with John and Osborne to Frøya for about a year, then settled in the larger city of Trondheim. A skilled seamstress, she opened a dress shop in the city. The shop, together with a lifetime pension and a short-term pension for John, helped to support them.[18]

In the meantime, John Andreas began an education that would provide the basis for his future profession. Until John was nine, some of John Andersen's former colleagues tutored the young boy. Precocious from an early age, John learned to read by age five. He read voraciously, and Shakespeare's *Merchant of Venice* particularly enchanted him as did the history and sagas of Norway. Through reading and contemplation, he developed an aversion to royal and dictatorial government even though Norway had been a constitutional monarchy in various forms since 1814. At about age nine, he entered a preparatory Latin school, and frequently spent summer school vacation in Frøya with his mother's family and friends.[19]

In Trondheim, however, Anna needed to have soles on John's worn shoes replaced, and she took them to Olaus Johnsen, a cobbler, whom friends had recommended. After he had replaced the

---

16. Widtsoe, *Gospel Net*, 56–57.
17. Widtsoe, *Gospel Net*, 58.
18. Widtsoe, *Gospel Net*, 59–61.
19. Widtsoe, *Gospel Net*, 60–61; Widtsoe, *Sunlit Land*, 4–5.

soles on John's shoes, Johnsen put Latter-day Saint tracts in each of them. As a Lutheran, Anna was at first reluctant to listen to the message conveyed by Johnsen's tracts. Upon learning that Johnsen belonged to the Church of Jesus Christ of Latter-day Saints—the Mormons—she recoiled with fright. In the nineteenth century, the Mormons had an extremely tawdry reputation in both Europe and the United States. Stories of polygamy, Danites, and avenging angels passed from mouth to mouth, and they appeared in the press, in articles, and in books. Nevertheless, she eventually agreed to attend church in the Trondheim branch that met in Johnsen's home. She listened to sermons and lessons from Elder Anthon L. Skanchy, and what Anna heard answered many of the questions she had pondered about this life and the next. After two years of studying the LDS gospel, Anna came to believe that she had heard the truth. She accepted baptism on April 1, 1881, and joined the small group of Saints in Trondheim.[20]

Even though John was nine at the time of her baptism, Anna declined to encourage him to present himself for baptism. She wanted John to "postpone baptism until I understood the gospel myself." Anna was convinced that "she must not influence me unduly."[21]

Joining a small group that most Norwegians considered a vile sect led to conflicts with Anna's family, friends, and Lutheran church leaders. Many previously close friends shunned Anna, and the local priest threatened to try to revoke her pension. She was particularly disappointed that her unmarried sister, Petroline Gaarden, to whom she had been particularly close, declined at the time to join the church. She feared also that her decision to convert to the Latter-day Saints might endanger the future prospects of her two young sons.[22]

She learned of a way, however, to mitigate that danger. In the nineteenth century and well into the twentieth, most converts who lived outside of the American Mountain West dreamed of gathering to LDS settlements in Utah. Church leaders encouraged such a

---

20. Widtsoe, *Gospel Net*, 65–68; Widtsoe, *Sunlit Land*, 7.
21. Widtsoe, *Sunlit Land*, 6.
22. Widtsoe, *Gospel Net*, 68–70, 72.

gathering, and Anna planned to take her two boys with her to Zion, but she lacked the finances.

By 1883 she had saved some money, and three elders—Anthon L Skancy, who had baptized her; Christian H. Steffensen; and Ole Berkhoel—contributed to her emigration fund. John was eleven and Osborne five when she arranged to take them with her. Petroline had no reason to emigrate with her because she was not a Latter-day Saint. To prepare to leave, Anna sold her furniture and auctioned off most of her late husband's library.[23]

The three left Norway in October 1883. Sailing first to Hull, England, they traveled by rail to Liverpool where they boarded the *S. S. Wisconsin*. After sailing to New York City, they took the train to Logan, Utah, arriving in mid-November 1883.[24]

Even though John was eleven, because of his lack of skill in English, the school authorities placed him in the second grade. Within a week they recognized the extent of his Latin school education, but instead of advancing him to the sixth grade where he would have studied with his age group, they placed him in the seventh.[25]

Osborne was only six years old so he could not work, but Anna and eleven-year-old John had to support the family. John worked at various odd jobs such as stacking firewood, building roads, clearing wheat bins, delivering milk, farming, and newspaper printing. He finally landed a job at the United Order store, Logan's largest general store. Working as a clerk, he got to know nearly everyone in Logan.[26]

Since most people in the community were Latter-day Saints, the initial language barrier offered few problems in developing friendships with others. Moreover, John learned English rapidly because of his young age, his experiences with English-speaking friends, and his studies in school. John also developed a number of lasting friendships with other Logan boys. These included James Z. Stewart Jr.; Guy B. Thatcher; John H. Squires; Joseph Quinney Jr.; and Joseph E. Cardon. With the other boys, he organized study and debate clubs, played baseball, and engaged in field activities such as running and jumping.[27]

---

23. Widtsoe, *Gospel Net*, 74–75.
24. Widtsoe, *Gospel Net*, 76–77; Widtsoe, *Sunlit Land*, 8.
25. Widtsoe, *Sunlit Land*, 8.
26. Widtsoe, *Sunlit Land*, 8–9.
27. Widtsoe, *Sunlit Land*, 9–10.

The Widtsoes settled in the Logan First Ward. In April 1884, the year after they arrived, John asked to be baptized. He was twelve at the time, and shortly after baptism, he was ordained a deacon in the Aaronic Priesthood. Soon, the ward bishop called him to be secretary of the deacon's quorum. As a deacon, John participated in compassionate and service activities. He and other deacons chopped wood for widows and helped to prepare the room in the Logan Stake Tabernacle in which the First Ward held church services.[28]

During the 1880s, the church's meeting schedule was much different from today. The wards held Sunday school in the morning and sacrament meetings in the evening on Sundays and Aaronic and Melchizedek Priesthood meetings on Monday evenings. Until 1896, church wards held fast and testimony meeting on the morning of the first Thursdays of each month. Beginning in 1896, the church leadership shifted fast and testimony meeting to the first Sundays of each month. Each stake (composed of groups of wards) held stake conferences quarterly throughout the year. In the nineteenth and early twentieth centuries, a member of the First Presidency and someone from the Quorum of the Twelve Apostles or one of the First Seven Presidents of the Seventy attended the stake quarterly conferences.

Although the church organized the Young Men's Mutual Improvement Association in 1878, the Logan First Ward did not organize its YMMIA until 1886. Widtsoe helped to organize the first one in his ward.[29]

Widtsoe considered the 4,000–5,000 people in Logan to be "a veritable melting pot of nationalities." Though "a few Southern Europeans" lived in town, Logan was more accurately a melting pot of Northern Europeans and people who descended from Northern Europe.[30]

The 1880 census listed Logan's population as 3,396. The county seat of Cache County, Logan had grown 93.3 percent since 1870, and would increase to 4,565 or 34.4 percent by 1890. Nevertheless, the city had little official circulating specie, and Logan's citizens made most of their purchases with what Widtsoe called "store orders." Store orders were scrip similar to paper money since they appeared

---

28. Widtsoe, *Sunlit Land*, 10.
29. Widtsoe, *Sunlit Land*, 10–11.
30. Widtsoe, *Sunlit Land*, 13.

in various denominations. Stores rather than governments issued such scrip, however, and customers could use them in the stores that issued them. Some stores accepted the scrip of competitors, but like the paper money issued by banks before the passage of the national banking acts in 1863 to 1864, some of the stores and businesses refused to accept them or accepted them only at a discount. Scrip was, however, necessary in an economy like Utah's in the mid- to late-nineteenth century which had little official circulating medium.[31]

Logan had a railroad connection which gave it one advantage over some other small cities. LDS Church leaders and other investors had constructed the Utah and Northern Railroad to Logan in 1873.[32] The railroad went to Franklin, Idaho, a town in Cache Valley north of Logan. They intended to build it to Montana but could not secure the financing so sold it to Union Pacific by 1877.[33]

Logan had a normal mix of occupations, but like many small towns in Utah and elsewhere, most residential lots had enough space for vegetable and fruit gardens and some sheds and coops to house farm animals, such as chickens and cows. John and Osborne tended the garden. For them and many of those who had come from foreign cities, keeping a garden was a new experience. With the exception of local bankers like the Thatcher brothers and a doctor, most people in late-nineteenth-century Logan lived in a range of relative middle-class equality.[34]

In addition to the elementary schools, late-nineteenth-century Logan had two colleges. LDS Church president Brigham Young chartered Brigham Young College in Logan in 1877, shortly before his death. Although called a "College," it was principally a high school. Brigham Young College closed in 1926, and the church donated its buildings to Logan to use as a high school. In 1890, the Agricultural College of Utah (renamed Utah State Agricultural College in 1929, and Utah State University in 1957) admitted its

---

31. Widtsoe, *Sunlit Land*, 13; Leonard J. Arrington, *Great Basin Kingdom: A History of the Latter-day Saints, 1830–1900* (Cambridge, MA: Harvard University Press, 1958), 312–13, 497nn88–89.

32. Widtsoe, *Sunlit Land*, 12.

33. Arrington, *Great Basin Kingdom*, 287–88.

34. Widtsoe, *Sunlit Land*, 13–14, 15–17.

first students. Unlike Brigham Young College, the AC, as it was known, has operated continuously since then.

Logan had a number of activities and establishments to provide the citizens with entertainment and relaxation. The Logan Tabernacle featured a stake choir. Celebrations took place on July 4th and 24th to commemorate, respectively, Independence Day and Pioneer Day (when the LDS pioneers entered the Salt Lake Valley in 1847). The city had saloons and a billiard hall to furnish entertainment for those so inclined.[35]

The psychological distance for Widtsoe from Frøyan and Trondheim to Logan was not as great as one might expect. John Andersen's death dislocated the family for some time, but with the help of friends and relatives, Anna and her two sons made the best of a difficult, challenging situation. By joining the LDS Church, Anna created a chasm between herself and her family and former friends. Nevertheless, in Logan the Widtsoe family joined a community of like-minded Saints, most of whom descended from Northern Europeans or immigrated from Northern Europe.

The decision to emigrate from Norway placed a bandage on the hurt she and her boys felt because she had left the state church. Moreover, since Anna and her sons traveled in a company of Latter-day Saints, the trip itself proved less painless than for immigrants who might have traveled alone or with a single family. When the Widtsoe family reached Logan, they became part of a covenant community that took them in and helped in their relocation. The family moved into a house with a garden, and both John and Anna found employment. John began school in Logan, learned to speak English, and demonstrated his intelligence and ability so rapidly that he advanced in school faster than some Logan-born children. The immigration experience proved beneficial for John and his family.

---

35. Widtsoe, *Sunlit Land*, 14–15.

CHAPTER TWO

EDUCATION AND ADVANCEMENT

In the late-nineteenth century, many—perhaps most—Americans considered high schools as strictly preparatory academies for students who intended to go to college. As a result, many children completed their education in the eighth grade, and far too many did not attend school that long. For the Widtsoes, whose father who had graduated from a *seminarium* and the University of Oslo, neither of these choices appealed. The Widtsoe family assumed that John and Osborne would follow in their father's footsteps, graduate from college, and become teachers.

John prepared for this future by continuing his voracious reading. During his youth, Logan, Utah, had only one bookstore. James T. Hammond, who later served as Utah's secretary of state, owned the store. Widtsoe was a friend and frequent customer.[1]

Because of his employment in the co-op, Widtsoe decided to drop out of public school. In place of school, he read voraciously, taught himself, and engaged private tutors for instruction in various subjects after work. He studied Latin and English with W. H. Apperley who joined the faculty of Brigham Young College. He taught himself arithmetic and the rudiments of algebra.[2]

By the time Widtsoe turned seventeen, the family had become solvent and he could attend high school. By then, the Widtsoes owned their own home, and their garden supplied most of their food. Anna continued to work in the profession she had followed

---

1. John A. Widtsoe, *In a Sunlit Land: The Autobiography of John A. Widtsoe* (Salt Lake City: Milton R. Hunter and G. Homer Durham, 1952), 19, 20.
2. Widtsoe, *Sunlit Land*, 20.

in Trondheim and helped to support the family by making dresses for other women. Widtsoe, himself, decided that the family could probably support itself if he worked only on Saturdays and in the late afternoon and evening, instead of working full time.[3]

In the fall term 1889, after he had concluded that the family could get along with his part-time work, he enrolled in high school at Brigham Young College. Although named Brigham Young College, the school was basically a high school much like the other schools throughout the LDS Church called academies. He understood that Brigham Young College had poor library and laboratory facilities and that most of the teachers lacked advanced degrees from accredited universities, but he discovered that many of them had mastered their subjects and could teach with "excellence." He studied with a number of teachers including Douglas M. Todd, William H. Smart, W. H. Apperley, F. K. Nebeker, and Joseph M. Tanner. Tanner, who taught theology, was college president at the time. Widtsoe studied theology, rhetoric, German, Latin, physics chemistry, geology, bookkeeping, algebra, geometry, and educational theory. Although Widtsoe was an undergraduate, in his second year Tanner hired him to teach "beginning" algebra. Widtsoe was particularly pleased to have studied the Bible, and he advocated education in religion (outside of public schools) and ethics (in public schools), in addition to secular subjects.[4]

Widtsoe and his classmates were not above playing pranks. Widtsoe joined with others in one caper with a teacher who walked very slowly as their target. Using a fact they learned in chemistry, the boys placed some nitrogen iodide on the steps leading from the teacher's room in the school building's basement to the main floor instruction area. As the targeted teacher trod on each step, the substance exploded under his shoes. As the nitrogen iodide exploded, the eruption induced him to hasten upward.[5]

Widtsoe and his friends' knowledge of chemistry played a role in another prank. One June afternoon, they entered a barbershop on the west side of Main Street across from the Logan Tabernacle.

3. Widtsoe, *Sunlit Land*, 20–21.
4. Widtsoe, *Sunlit Land*, 21–22, 24–25.
5. Widtsoe, *Sunlit Land*, 22.

They drilled a hole through the wall of the barbershop and into an adjacent clothing store that was owned by a Jewish tailor. After running a tube through the hole, they attached a bottle of rotten egg gas (hydrogen disulphide) which flowed into the store. An "unspeakable stench" from the gas filled the clothing store. The gas drove the employees out of the store and flowed onto the adjacent sidewalk, where it irritated those who passed by including the city's mayor. After citizens discovered what Widtsoe and the other culprits had done, city officials made them apologize. Later, in writing about the incident, however, Widtsoe made it clear that their apology was anything but sincere.[6]

Widtsoe graduated from "the intermediate grade" at Brigham Young College in June 1891, and left the same month by train for Cambridge, Massachusetts, in the company of Joseph Jenson. Both expected to enroll at Harvard. To pay partly for his education, Widtsoe borrowed $1,500 from the bank for which he signed a mortgage on the family home at 12 percent interest. He also secured loans from local citizens: John E. Carlisle, B. F. Riter, H. H. Thain, Isaac Smith, and A. L. Skanchy.

Widtsoe and Jenson joined a number of other Latter-day Saint students who enrolled in schools in Cambridge and Boston that year. Joseph M. Tanner left Brigham Young College to study law at Harvard. Since he was born in 1859, Tanner was older than the other students. To help accommodate the large number of students from Utah, Tanner rented a home so he and the young men and women could live more cheaply. In three subsequent years, Tanner rented different homes to house the students.[7]

Widtsoe remembered seventeen students who lived in Tanner's homes. Most of them studied at Harvard, but some were enrolled at Massachusetts Institute of Technology and the New England Conservatory of Music. Widtsoe remarked that each of those who studied in the Boston area that year achieved notable positions after they completed their education. Widtsoe's contemporaries included George Thomas, later president of the University of Utah; Joseph Jenson and Caleb Tanner, who became Utah State Engineers; Lewis

---

6. Widtsoe, *Sunlit Land*, 23–24.
7. Widtsoe, *Sunlit Land*, 28–29.

T. Cannon, who practiced as a noted architect; and Arthur Shepherd, who achieved international fame as a composer.[8]

Before he could enroll in Harvard, Widtsoe had to pass an entrance examination. He knew that some of the classes he had studied and some he had taken at Brigham Young College helped him to prepare for the exam, but that he needed further study to pass. During the remainder of the summer of 1891, he took a course in German, and he taught himself trigonometry and analytic geometry. Widtsoe not only passed the examination but earned a sufficiently high enough grade in one of the subjects to receive credit toward graduation from Harvard.[9]

When deciding on a major, Widtsoe chose from among mathematics, English, and chemistry. A practical problem weighed heavily on his mind as he made his decision. He knew that he would have to care for Anna, Aunt Petroline, and Osborne, until his younger brother could support himself. With chemistry, he reasoned, he could teach or work in mining or manufacturing. With math and English, he believed his choices of occupations were more limited. On balance, however, he did not choose chemistry entirely from practical considerations. Chemistry attracted him because he wanted to understand the chemical aspects of everything in the universe.[10]

Widtsoe found chemistry exciting and fulfilling. He particularly reveled in doing research. One project exposed him to history and archaeology. In this study, he analyzed the chemical composition of ancient pottery to determine whether it was made in ancient Greece or Egypt. While working on research in organic chemistry during his senior year, he discovered compounds possibly never before known to science. Others recognized Widtsoe as a high achiever by electing him president of the chemistry department's only club, the Boylston Chemical Club, during his senior year.[11]

During the years Widtsoe studied at Harvard, the university's chemistry department boasted some of the field's leading lights. These included Theodore W. Richards, who later earned a Nobel

8. Widtsoe, *Sunlit Land*, 28–29.
9. Widtsoe, *Sunlit Land*, 30–31.
10. Widtsoe, *Sunlit Land*, 31.
11. Widtsoe, *Sunlit Land*, 32.

Prize for developing the method to determine the atomic weights of elements. Richards used the method he invented to find the weights of a large number of the chemicals. Others in the department included Henry B. Hill and Charles L. Jackson, who were excellent teachers and researchers.[12]

Widtsoe, however, was most impressed by the department chair, Josiah Parsons Cooke. Widtsoe wrote that Cooke took "a special interest" in him and "influenced my life greatly." Cooke rejected the views of some that religion and science necessarily conflicted with each other. The older chemist believed that all "of nature was but God's speech," and he frequently expressed that belief in lectures to popular audiences.[13]

Widtsoe found his association with Cooke particularly significant because, during his four years at Harvard, he struggled with his faith. He wondered whether Mormonism really was "what it pretended to be." He did not give himself over to positivism and naturalism, but rather he "read, listened, compared, thought, and prayed." As a mentor, Cooke helped Widtsoe to reconcile his faith with his commitment to the scientific method. He invited Widtsoe to his "great library," he talked with the young man "about the philosophy and the mystery of life and the best manner of picking one's way among contending doctrines." Cooke's faith in the congruence of religion and science "was a great help ... in finding my way to spiritual truth." Because of Cooke's mentorship, Widtsoe confessed that "I owe much to" him.[14]

Although Widtsoe majored in chemistry, he had also developed a deep love for the English language and literature. His lifelong love for reading and his practice of reading widely in various genres of English literature helped to improve his writing style, and throughout his life he wrote in his adopted language with clarity and style. Widtsoe enjoyed reading poetry, especially the work of his older contemporary Alfred Lord Tennyson, who served as British Poet

---

12. Widtsoe, *Sunlit Land*, 36; nobelprize.org (accessed Feb. 1, 2021).

13. Widtsoe, *Sunlit Land*, 36–37.

14. Widtsoe, *Sunlit Land*, 36–37. Personally, I owe a great deal to two professors who were active Latter-day Saints: S. George Ellsworth and Leonard J. Arrington, each of whom set an example as a first-rate teacher and scholar and as a faithful Latter-day Saint during the years I studied under them and later as a colleague.

Laureate from 1850 to 1892. He also expanded his familiarity with English literature in L. B. R. Briggs's class on Shakespeare. Widtsoe's ease and fluency in English were evident in articles he wrote for the *Harvard Crimson* newspaper and the *Harvard Advocate*, an art and literary magazine. Others, including the editors of the *Boston Herald*, who republished one of his stories, recognized his gift for writing.

Widtsoe broadened his education by taking classes in other subjects. He considered philosopher William James "famous and lovable," though because James had a stomach ulcer that year, he thought the man "lived in a dark and uninviting universe." This seems an odd way to evaluate a man who was perhaps America's leading pragmatist and who considered religion to be an important aspect of human culture. On reflection, it seems probable that Widtsoe's views about James may have been influenced by his experience at Harvard rather than by James's later writing on religion, especially the Gifford Lectures.[15]

Widtsoe thought Josiah Royce "great," but he was unconvinced by Royce's notion of Absolute Idealism. Widtsoe could not believe, as Royce taught, that "that all aspects of reality, including those we experience as disconnected or contradictory, are ultimately unified in the thought of a single all-encompassing consciousness."[16]

Significantly, Widtsoe was taken aback the first time he saw Royce because he was so short. He did not recognize the diminutive Royce the first time he saw him on the street, and he had to re-think his own prejudices when he saw the man's obvious brilliance in the classroom. This insight led Widtsoe to conclude that he should never judge someone by his or her "outward appearances."[17]

Widtsoe gained other insights from his experience at Harvard. He took geology from N. S. Shaler, zoology from E. L. Mark, and physics from E. H. Hall. Outside of the chemistry department, Widtsoe was most impressed by President Charles W. Eliot, a renowned chemist before he became university president. Widtsoe considered him "easily the foremost citizen of America" of his

---

15. Widtsoe, *Sunlit Land*, 34. See William James, *The Varieties of Religious Experience* ... (London: Longmans Green, 1902).

16. *Stanford Encyclopedia of Philosophy* at plato.stanford.edu (accessed Feb. 2, 2021); Widtsoe, *Sunlit Land*, 34–35.

17. Widtsoe, *Sunlit Land*, 34–35.

generation. In addition to the classes he took, Widtsoe increased his knowledge and satisfied his interests by spending considerable time browsing in the university's Gore Hall library.[18]

A curious student with wide-ranging interests, Widtsoe also used his free time to participate in cultural activities. He believed that Boston was "the cultural centre of America." He attended a number of theater performances and lectures. He saw a performance by the actor Joseph Jefferson. The play he saw was probably *Rip Van Winkle*, Jefferson's most famous, most frequently performed role. Widtsoe thrilled to the noted French actress, Sarah Bernhardt—most likely during her world tour of 1891 to 1893 since she was in Paris during the years before 1891 and after 1893. Widtsoe wrote that he also attended lectures by "famous men."[19]

On June 12, 1894, Widtsoe stood for his honors exam. In the exam, he reported on his research work and wrote details about it on the blackboard. He explained how disulphuric acid, ($H_2S_2O_7$), also called pyrosulphuric acid and oleum, is made. Disulphuric Acid is a chemical used, among other things, to coat the inside of metal tanks to protect them from corrosion while transporting sulphuric acid. He also "discussed sugar analysis" as part of the exam. After completing the exam, he was quite nervous but learned after waiting for the afternoon that he had graduated with "highest honors" (*summa cum laude*).[20]

The university recognized Widtsoe's ability and later his outstanding accomplishments. As he finished his education, the professors offered him a laboratory assistantship, a position in a chemical company, or work in the Rand South African gold mines. Instead of taking those offers, he accepted a position at the Utah State Agricultural College in Logan, Utah. In recognition of his lifetime achievement, in 1944, after the Second World War had turned in the Allies' favor, Harvard invited him to speak at the 50th anniversary of his graduation.[21]

While in Cambridge, in addition to attending school and participating in cultural activities, as he struggled with his faith, Widtsoe

---

18. Widtsoe, *Sunlit Land*, 34–35.
19. Widtsoe, *Sunlit Land*, 35–36.
20. Widtsoe, *Sunlit Land*, 32–33, 40.
21. Widtsoe, *Sunlit Land*, 40–41.

continued his activity in the LDS Church. Today the church has more than 16 million members. In 1894, the year Widtsoe graduated from Harvard, the church had just over 324,000 members, most of whom lived in Utah and surrounding states.[22] In 1894, the church had twenty-five general authorities, including the First Presidency, the Twelve Apostles, the First Council of the Seventy, and the Presiding Bishopric. All were Caucasian men and all had been residing in the Mountain West, principally in Utah, at the times of their callings to church leadership. By contrast, at the October 2020 General Conference, church members sustained 239 general authorities, including the First Presidency, the Twelve Apostles, the Presidency of the Seventy, the General Authority Seventies, and the Presiding Bishopric. In addition to Caucasians, in 2020, the LDS general authorities included Hispanics, Asians, and Africans. Many came from outside the Mountain West, and a number lived in foreign countries in Europe, Africa, South America, and Asia at the time of their calling.[23]

Since so many Latter-day Saints, especially young men (and some women), lived in 1892 in what Widtsoe called the "little Mormon colony," a number of prominent Latter-day Saints and general authorities visited the students. During these visits, as Widtsoe noted, he and the others made "acquaintanceships" that "often lasted through life and grew into friendships." LDS officials George Q. Cannon and Moses Thatcher had particular reasons for visiting because they had sons in the university. Widtsoe mentions others who visited Cambridge, including R. K. Thomas, a Salt Lake City merchant, and his future mother-in-law, Susa Young Gates.[24]

During the late-nineteenth and early-twentieth centuries, the relationship between Harvard and women was complex. Harvard sponsored some summer schools for women during the years Widtsoe attended, but women could not enroll during the year in regular classes. Breaking with tradition in 1920, Harvard's graduate school of education began admitting women. Until 1963, however, women

---

22. Deseret News, *2001–2002 Church Almanac* (Salt Lake City: Deseret News, 2001), 583.

23. *Ensign*, Nov. 2020, 64–65.

24. Widtsoe, *Sunlit Land*, 38–39.

could attend Radcliffe and, as a concession, the president of Harvard co-signed their diplomas. In 1963 Harvard awarded undergraduate degrees to women from Radcliffe for the first time.[25]

The special summer classes created an unusual opportunity for women. In 1892, Susa Young Gates, Brigham Young's strong-willed daughter, traveled to Cambridge where she met with Maud May Babcock who had been teaching summer courses in physical education at Harvard since 1890. While in Cambridge, Gates recruited Babcock to move to Salt Lake City to teach physical education and speech at the University of Utah. Babcock moved to the U of U where she established the departments of speech and of physical education. The speech department included drama, and Babcock produced more than 300 plays during her tenure at the university.[26]

In the summer of 1893, however, Babcock returned to Harvard to teach a class in physical education. She brought with her from Utah a number of women in addition to Gates. These included Gates's daughter Leah Eudora Dunford and Mae Taylor, Belle Salmon, and Kate Thomas. Widtsoe had met Gates the previous year, but the summer of 1893 was his first meeting with Leah Dunford, whom he married in 1898. Widtsoe later said that 1893 "was a truly delightful summer, for it was then that two young hearts learned to understand the language of love." He considered Babcock "the fairy godmother of our later union," who "always had an honored place in our family."[27]

After departing Cambridge, Widtsoe left by train for Salt Lake City. The 1894 Pullman strike delayed his train in Ohio and Chicago. The experience left him with a lifelong anti-union bent. He met his family in Salt Lake City before they all returned to Logan.[28]

The years between 1889 and 1894 were important because they set Widtsoe on the path he was to follow until his calling to the Quorum of the Twelve Apostles, and to some degree even after that call. Widtsoe had prepared for college by tutoring himself and receiving instruction in various high school subjects. He became

---

25. See news.harvard.edu (accessed Feb. 4, 2021).

26. Widtsoe, *Sunlit Land*, 38.

27. Widtsoe, *Sunlit Land*, 39–40. See also Romney Burke, *Susa Young Gates: Daughter of Mormonism* (Salt Lake City: Signature Books, 2022) *passim*.

28. Widtsoe, *Sunlit Land*, 41.

acquainted with Joseph M. Tanner, who helped to further his career at the Agricultural College of Utah. He met frequently with Josiah M. Cooke, chair of Harvard's chemistry department, who helped him work through his doubts about the congruence of science and religion and he worked through questions of faith. He also met a number of young men and women who became community leaders in Utah and elsewhere. Of special importance, he met and began to court Leah Eudora Dunford, whom he eventually married. Perhaps most important for his future education, he graduated *summa cum laude*, which put him on the track for a future professorial position, research success, and an education at Göttingen, one of Europe's foremost universities, where he would earn a PhD in chemistry.

CHAPTER THREE

UTAH STATE AGRICULTURAL COLLEGE AND GERMANY

Congressional acts of 1862 and 1888 established the United States' land grant college system and authorized the establishment of experiment stations. The 1862 act, sponsored by Congressman Justin S. Morrill of Vermont, authorized a grant of 30,000 acres of public land for each congressman elected from every state to establish an agricultural college in the state. In 1888 Congress authorized each state to establish an experiment station in connection with the college. Until the Second Morrill Act of 1890 provided additional appropriations from Congress for agricultural colleges, the states and territories provided much of the support for the colleges.[1]

Representative Anthon H. Lund of Sanpete County, a Danish immigrant who later became a member of the First Presidency of the LDS Church, introduced legislation that the Utah territorial legislature approved in 1888 to establish an agricultural college in Utah. Because of a compromise, in a three-way conflict the legislature placed the college in Logan, established a reform school in Ogden, and founded a state mental hospital in Provo. Both Ogden and Provo thought they got the best of the deal because they expected the college to be very small and less important than the reform school or the mental hospital, but the legislature appropriated more money for the college than it did for the other institutions. Logan, some eighty-three miles north of Salt Lake City, prospered as a result.[2]

---

1. Roger L. Geiger and Nathan M. Sorber, eds., *The Land-Grant Colleges and the Reshaping of American Higher Education* (New York: Routledge, 2013), *passim.*

2. John A. Widtsoe, *In a Sunlit Land: The Autobiography of John A. Widtsoe* (Salt Lake City: Milton R. Hunter and G. Homer Durham, 1952), 44–45.

In 1894, the year Widtsoe joined the agricultural college faculty, Joshua H. Paul, a Latter-day Saint, succeeded non-Mormon, Jeremiah W. Sanborn, as Utah State Agricultural College (USAC) president. Widtsoe had high regard for both men, but anti-Mormonism soon reared its ugly head. In 1894 Widtsoe and Paul were the only Latter-day Saints in the faculty's collegiate division. During the 1894–95 school year, "one of the leading members of the faculty" cornered Widtsoe. He told Widtsoe that members of the faculty had held "a private meeting" and voted to ask him to resign. They were going to try to get Paul to resign also so the faculty would be free of any potential Mormon influence. He said that he considered Mormons a "blemish" on the institution. Undaunted, Widtsoe told him that he would remain on the faculty "'until every one who sent the request had left the institution.'" In Widtsoe's view, competence rather than intolerance should govern the decision over faculty and administration at an institution of learning. The institution, he wrote, should be "dedicated to the discovery and dissemination of truth."[3]

Widtsoe spent the first summer after he returned to Utah teaching at a six-week session in a teacher's institute. He taught chemistry to educators but would rather have engaged in experimental research. His appointment to the faculty of the agricultural college included an assignment as the experiment station's chemist. In Widtsoe's view and in the perception of many others, since agriculture begins with the soil, it was important to determine "the nature of Utah's soils." Some critics believed that Widtsoe should confine this research to the college's farms, but President Paul authorized him to investigate the composition of soils throughout Utah. As a result, Widtsoe traveled to various counties in the state making observations and taking soil samples, which he analyzed to determine their chemical and biochemical composition. He published the results of his research in experiment station bulletins and in chemical journals. Through this research Widtsoe discovered that Utah had some soils of "astonishing fertility." His chemical analysis "led to the formulation of suitable cropping systems" for various areas throughout the state.[4]

Widtsoe conducted research on various plants to determine their

3. Widtsoe, *Sunlit Land*, 45–47.
4. Widtsoe, *Sunlit Land*, 41, 47–48.

adaptability for propagation in Utah soils. One of these was alfalfa, a plant most Utahns called lucern. Farmers generally grew lucern to store as hay to feed to herbivore animals, especially cows and horses, during Utah's harsh winters. Before wrapping alfalfa into bails became the general practice, farmers in Utah generally stacked the lucern with derricks either on the ground or in lofts in barns. When Widtsoe returned to Utah in 1894, however, he knew that although lucern "was the foremost crop" grown in Utah, farmers and scientists understood "very little … concerning the composition and growth habits of the crop." To bridge the gaps in this knowledge, Widtsoe spent three years studying lucern. In his research, he determined lucern's rate of growth, its composition at various stages of growth, and the effect of the plant on the "growth and well-being of livestock." He published the research in several experiment station bulletins; practical farmers generally accepted his findings.[5]

Widtsoe also conducted similar research on sugar beets. Unlike lucern, which nineteenth- and early-twentieth-century farmers generally grew for consumption by their own livestock, farmers grew sugar beets as a major cash crop. With the construction of a plant in Lehi, Utah, in 1891 and the subsequent erection of similar plants throughout the Intermountain West, companies including the Utah-Idaho and Amalgamated Sugar companies contracted with farmers to grow sugar beets. Wagons, and later trucks, transported the beets from Utah farms to the plants in which the companies extracted the sweet content of the beets and transformed it into sugar which they marketed. Widtsoe contributed to the success of the industry through two years of experimentation on small plots of sugar beets in which he demonstrated that farmers could grow sugar beets "successfully everywhere in the State."[6]

In addition to this research, Widtsoe played a significant role in originating agricultural extension work in Utah. In agricultural extension work, the state established agents in multiple counties to assist farmers and sponsored classes on various subjects, often at

---

5. Widtsoe, *Sunlit Land*, 48.

6. Leonard J. Arrington, *Beet Sugar in the West: A History of the Utah-Idaho Sugar Company, 1891–1966* (Seattle: University of Washington Press, 1966), *passim*; J. R. Bachman, *Story of the Amalgamated Sugar Company, 1897–1961* (Caldwell, ID: Caxton Printers, 1962), *passim*; Widtsoe, *Sunlit Land*, 48.

meetings called institutes, to help farmers carry on their agricultural businesses more efficiently and successfully. Because of a legislative appropriation of $1,500 in 1895, agricultural college president Joseph M. Tanner and F. B. Linfield, a professor of dairy, held farmers' institutes in various portions of the state. In 1897 Widtsoe and Joseph Jenson, a professor of mechanical engineering, conducted similar farmers' institutes in most Utah towns south of Provo. Widtsoe recognized that these were the earliest efforts to establish agricultural extension programs and offices in the state.[7]

During the 1897 trip with Jenson, Widtsoe learned much about the geography of the desert region of Utah. In this pre-automobile age, the two scholars traveled by horse-drawn wagon. Widtsoe noted the soil and plants as they traveled. On this journey, they crossed Utah's southern border into Arizona, where they reached Point Sublime on the Grand Canyon. On this and subsequent trips, Widtsoe gained some understanding of the "rich geological history of the region." Widtsoe recognized not only the West's beauty, but also "the history of immense periods of earth making ... [in the geologic] phases of ocean and desert."[8]

During the years between 1894 and 1898, in addition to holding farmers' institutes and traveling throughout Utah, Widtsoe continued his research on agricultural chemistry, more particularly what was then called physiological chemistry and more recently biochemistry. That is, he sought to determine the chemical "processes within living plants, animals and humans." Presidents Paul and Tanner both provided active support for Widtsoe's biochemical research.[9]

Widtsoe quickly realized that his current knowledge had limits and that to advance his research, he would have to study with scholars who knew more than he did. He understood, also, that the world's preeminent biochemical scholars resided in Europe. To further his education, he applied for and received one of Harvard's four Parker traveling fellowships. He used this fellowship to support himself and his family while he studied at the University of Göttingen in north-central Germany.[10]

---

7. Widtsoe, *Sunlit Land*, 49.
8. Widtsoe, *Sunlit Land*, 49–50.
9. Widtsoe, *Sunlit Land*, 52–53.
10. Widtsoe, *Sunlit Land*, 53.

Although Widtsoe applied for the fellowship as a bachelor, he indeed planned to travel with his family because on June 1, 1898, he married Leah Eudora Dunford (b. 1874), whom he had courted since they met five years earlier in Cambridge. The daughter of Susa Young Dunford—later Gates—and Alma Dunford, a Salt Lake City dentist, Leah had studied at Maud May Babcock's physical education summer school at Harvard in 1893. While in Cambridge, she met and fell in love with Widtsoe. In an oral history interview, Leah said that when she traveled to Massachusetts, she had been writing to "'a tall, brown-eyed fellow ... in Utah,'" but in Cambridge she became so enamored of Widtsoe that she "'never wrote any more letters to him [the brown-eyed fellow].'"[11] In addition to studying in Babcock's summer classes, she majored in physical education at the University of Utah's Normal School from which she graduated as class valedictorian in 1896. After graduating, she became interested in nursing but grew dissatisfied with that profession because she could not understand why some people became sick. After making a decision not to become a nurse, she consulted with others including Maria Parloa and Fannie Farmer who operated famous cooking schools and Susan B. Anthony who, in addition to leading the nation's woman suffrage movement, promoted women's education.

Following this consultation and considerable study, Leah decided to enroll in classes in domestic science and domestic arts at the Pratt Institute in Brooklyn, New York. Donetta Smith, a daughter of LDS Church president Joseph F. Smith, enrolled in the Pratt Institute's kindergarten program at the same time, so the two of them traveled together. Leah had studied some aspects of domestic science at the University of Utah under James E. Talmage, who wrote a book on the subject. Because of her previous preparation, she succeeded in completing the Pratt Institute's course in one year.[12]

Through her mother's influence with Brigham Young Academy's (later Brigham Young University) president, Benjamin Cluff, Leah obtained permission to teach domestic science and to establish the Department of Home Economics at the academy. The BYA

11. Quoted in Alan K. Parrish, *John A. Widtsoe: A Biography* (Salt Lake City: Deseret Book Co., 2003), 100.
12. Parrish, *John A. Widtsoe*, 101.

administration created a rudimentary laboratory for the department in the building on lower campus (now part of the Provo City Library at Academy Square). During the 1897 to 1898 year, Dunford taught twelve classes in subjects such as cooking, home nursing, home economics, marketing, laundry, and dietetics. Because of her marriage to Widtsoe and their departure for Göttingen in the summer of 1898, Leah could not continue to offer courses in the department she had established.[13]

Widtsoe and Leah traveled to Germany by way of England and Holland. Accompanying them was Leah's sister Emma Lucy Gates (who later married Albert E. Bowen of the LDS Church's Quorum of the Twelve Apostles). Emma Lucy came to Germany to study music. The party landed in Liverpool in August 1898. At the time, Liverpool was the headquarters of the British and European Missions of the LDS Church. From Liverpool, they traveled to Leicester where they visited the H. B. Bruce family. Bruce was a wealthy rubber band manufacturer, and Mrs. Bruce was Leah's great aunt. From England, they traveled by boat from Harwich to Hook of Holland.

After arriving in Hook, the party became separated as they had misplaced Lucy's trunk. Widtsoe found it on a flatboat anchored on the Rhine, but before he had retrieved it, the train on which they were to ride to Göttingen had left with Leah and Emma Lucy. Notified of Widtsoe's situation, the two women managed to get off at a subsequent stop, and he took a local *Bummelzug* and caught up with them after which they continued to Göttingen together.[14]

Widtsoe apparently had little understanding of the range of local dialects in Germany. The three of them spent the night in Neuss, a town on the Rhein west of Düsseldorf. Most of the people in Neuss spoke a *Platt Deutsch* dialect called Kölsch. Many Germans in the region from Bonn on the south to Neuss on the north spoke Kölsch rather than High German. Apparently unaware that many of the people of the region spoke Kölsch, and not High German, Widtsoe thought that "the Germans were so poorly educated as to have difficulty in understanding their own language!"[15]

---

13. Parrish, *John A. Widtsoe*, 102–3.
14. Widtsoe, *Sunlit Land*, 53, 61–63.
15. Widtsoe, *Sunlit Land*, 63. I know something of this dialect as I served both in

Widtsoe had decided to study and do research at Göttingen because of the fame in research and publication of Herr Geheimrath Professor Doctor Bernhard Tollens. Tollens had earned his PhD at Göttingen in 1864. After graduation, he engaged in chemical research at a bronze factory, at the University of Heidelberg, as well as the Charles-Adolphe Wurtz institute in Paris, and as chief of the chemical laboratory at the University of Coimbra in Portugal. In 1872 he returned to occupy a chair in chemistry at Göttingen. Tollens remained on Göttingen's faculty until his death in 1918. During his tenure at Göttingen, Tollens inaugurated ground-breaking research on carbohydrates. He discovered the chemical structure of several sugars, developed the world famous Tollens reagent, and published the path-breaking results of his research. Most scientists considered Tollens the world's principal authority on sugars, starches, and nitrogenous substances. Tollens directed the Agricultural-Chemical Laboratory at the University of Göttingen, and, in Widtsoe's estimation, "was an exquisite experimenter."[16]

Widtsoe thought that Göttingen was Germany's second oldest university, but it was actually much farther down the line. George II, King of England and Elector of Hannover, founded the University of Göttingen in 1734. Germany's first university, Heidelburg, was founded in 1386. Its second, Leipzig, was founded in 1409, and a number of other universities were founded in the fifteenth and sixteenth centuries.[17]

Regardless of its age, a number of Americans, lured by the university's fame in numerous fields, had sought advanced degrees at Göttingen. These included historian George Bancroft and poet Henry Wadsworth Longfellow.[18]

Moreover, at the time Göttingen was the leading university in Europe in the fields that Widtsoe planned to study and in which he intended to conduct biochemical research. Given Utah's needs, Widtsoe concluded that he must "become well acquainted with the carbohydrates—sugar and starches, and also protein—the

---

Düsseldorf and Cologne during my proselytizing mission for the LDS Church from 1956 to 1958.

16. Widtsoe, *Sunlit Land*, 55.
17. Widtsoe, *Sunlit Land*, 55.
18. See library.harvard.edu (accessed Apr. 28, 2021).

nitrogenous substances." As the world's authority on these substances, Tollens offered Widtsoe the expertise he needed to do additional research on Utah's crops.[19]

Widtsoe heaped effusive praise on Tollens. Tollens spoke German, French, and English fluently. Widtsoe said that as students did their research, Tollens "moved quickly from place to place, usually muttering words of help in the native language of the student." Tollens and the students filled "the laboratory ... with the spirit of discovery."[20]

Focusing on the field of carbohydrates—starches and sugars— Widtsoe decided to do the research for his dissertation on traganuth gum also called tragacaenuth. Traganuth was used in a number of industrial, medical, and artistic applications including as a herbal remedy for coughs and diarrhea, as a treatment for burns, as a binder in artists' pastels, and as an adhesive.

Widtsoe succeeded to classify tragacanth among other carbohydrates. He found that it was a methyl pentosan, which researchers had not expected. For Widtsoe, as a biochemist who specialized in plants, this discovery was important because methyl pentosans were widely distributed in the plant kingdom. In the research for his doctoral dissertation Widtsoe formulated a test to recognize pentosan substances. In developing this test, Widtsoe used a spectroscope, a "new method of detection" discovered in the late nineteenth century.[21]

As minors in his university curriculum, Widtsoe studied physics and mineralogy. Among other things, Widtsoe conducted research on the optical properties of the crystals of a number of organic substances that scientists had not previously studied.[22]

Since Widtsoe's dissertation broke new ground in carbohydrate research, it should not surprise us that he passed his doctoral exam *magna cum laude*. He took his final exam on November 20, 1899, in Göttingen University's aula. He wrote that sixteen or eighteen professors questioned him for two to three hours. A half hour after completing the exam, the university notified him not only of the excellence of his dissertation but also that he had received a certificate

---

19. Widtsoe, *Sunlit Land*, 55.
20. Widtsoe, *Sunlit Land*, 55.
21. Widtsoe, *Sunlit Land*, 56.
22. Widtsoe, *Sunlit Land*, 56–57.

that authorized him to teach in Germany and to work in the nation's chemical industry.[23]

While in Göttingen, the Widtsoes and Lucy were the only Latter-day Saints in the city. On Sundays, John, Leah, and Lucy held their own worship services and gospel study class. Occasionally local LDS missionaries would visit them, and the mission president, Arnold Schulthess, came once. Lewis T. Cannon, a friend of long-standing, visited them as he returned from his mission.[24]

Continental European governments tended to regulate the movement of people, citizens and foreigners alike, and the Widtsoes and most Americans found some of the customs disconcerting. In Germany the family had to register their moves with the *Standes-amt*. In Zürich John and Leah had to undergo a Swiss civil marriage because they had not brought their marriage certificate with them and could not prove they were married. In Germany, citizens learned to give way to army officers on the sidewalk. Candidates for student fraternities (*Studentenkorps* or *Bursenschaften*) had to duel as a condition of membership. As a result, since most upper-class university graduates were right-handed, upper class German men generally bore one or more scars on the left side of their face.[25]

At times, unusual events made differences with those not of their LDS faith quite evident. At a party given by Tollens to celebrate his appointment as *Geheimrath*, Lucy accompanied John because Leah was near to delivering their first child, Anna. A Prussian officer escorted Lucy to dinner. She refused a glass of wine, and, taken aback, the officer asked "What do you drink?" She replied, "Water." "Wasser! … Mein Gott, Wasser ist nicht zum trinken, es ist zum Waschen." "My God, water is not for drinking, it is for washing."[26]

A surprise to Widtsoe, they found themselves as Americans unpopular in every European country they visited. Generally, Widtsoe observed the opposition to Americans resulted from the severe defeat and loss of colonies the United States had recently inflicted on Spain in the Spanish-American War. Widtsoe reported that his

---

23. Widtsoe, *Sunlit Land*, 57.
24. Widtsoe, *Sunlit Land*, 67.
25. Widtsoe, *Sunlit Land*, 68–69.
26. Widtsoe, *Sunlit Land*, 66.

family and he were frequently taunted with comments like, "Our upstart nation had no right to do injury to a European kingdom like Spain, with a government dating back many centuries."[27]

He had more pleasant experiences as he visited family members in Norway during the summer before he took his final examinations. Family members, especially cousins, treated him with respect and honor.[28]

While in Germany, Widtsoe decided to write for LDS Church magazines. He penned some poetry under a pseudonym, but his basic interest was to write articles for a lay audience from a scientific perspective. He believed that "the scriptural proof of the truth of the gospel had been quite fully developed and was unanswerable." Later in his career he wrote scriptural articles, but "only by assignment."[29]

After completing the examination, Widtsoe thanked the professors, "notably Geheimrath Tollens," telegraphed his wife who was in Berlin, slept soundly, lunched with friends, and arranged for the publication of his dissertation. Afterward, he returned to Berlin where he had stayed with his family while conducting research there. Significantly, in the spring of 1899, Joseph F. Merrill, who also became a member of the Quorum of the Twelve Apostles, earned his PhD at Johns Hopkins University. Merrill and Widtsoe were the first men to have received a PhD in residence who were later called to the apostleship. (James E. Talmage, who also served in the quorum, had received a PhD from Illinois Wesleyan University in 1896 for non-resident work.)[30]

Widtsoe expanded his education before returning to the United States. Leah and their daughter, Anna, who had recently been born, remained in Berlin while he traveled to Göttingen to stand for his final exam. After returning to Berlin, he attended lectures by several renowned researchers, including Emil Fischer who had also been "working on the chemical constitution of sugars." From Berlin Widtsoe and his family traveled to Zürich where he studied with

---

27. Widtsoe, *Sunlit Land*, 69.

28. Widtsoe, *Sunlit Land*, 70.

29. Widtsoe, *Sunlit Land*, 66–67.

30. Casey Paul Griffiths, *Truth Seeker: The Life of Joseph F. Merrill, Scientist, Educator, and Apostle* (Provo, UT: Brigham Young University Religious Studies Center and Salt Lake City: Deseret Book Co., 2021); Widtsoe, *Sunlit Land*, 58.

Professor Doctor Ernst Schulze at the Eidgenössische Technische Hochschule Zürich. Schulze, a biochemist, was at the time studying proteins and amino acids. Widtsoe considered him "perhaps at that time the foremost student and expert" on proteins. Schulze had already earned the Liebig-Medal in silver, and in 1910 the University of Heidelberg awarded him an honorary doctorate in medicine.

Widtsoe credited Tollens and Schulze with expanding his knowledge in a number of ways. Tollens "taught me how to crystallize substances out of dark, viscid remains of the acid or alkali digestion of animal or plant substances.... Schulze taught me how to filter such sticky remains to obtain clear solutions for further work." Widtsoe believed that without these processes, the "knowledge of several branches of science would have been retarded." Reciprocally, he taught Schulze the method to make crystals he had learned from Tollens.[31]

After working with Schultz in Zürich, Widtsoe took Leah and Anna to London. They spent the spring and summer of 1899 in the British capitol. He spent most of his time in the museums, the British Library, and London University. He found the experience "profitable." In addition, he visited the Rothampsted Experiment Station where Dr. J. H. Gilbert took him to a sloping meadow where long strips of grasses had responded to different mixtures of plant foods by developing diverse colors.[32]

About a month before John, Leah, and Anna were to return to the United States, John learned that Joseph M. Tanner had resigned as USAC president. B. H. Roberts had been elected to Congress as a representative from Utah, however, they refused to seat him because Roberts practiced polygamy. Tanner resigned when Congress threatened to deny any appropriations for the agricultural college if a polygamist remained on the payroll.[33]

Tanner asked Widtsoe to apply for the college's presidency, which he did. Letters supporting his candidacy poured in from a number of supporters, including Charles W. Eliot, several Harvard professors, other nationally prominent educators, and his major professor at Göttingen, Bernhard Tollens. On the advice of a "valued friend and

---

31. Widtsoe, *Sunlit Land*, 58–59.
32. Widtsoe, *Sunlit Land*, 60.
33. Widtsoe, *Sunlit Land*, 70–71.

leader," Widtsoe declined the presidential appointment. Following his refusal, the board by a one-vote majority elected William J. Kerr, previously president of Logan's Brigham Young College, as president and Widtsoe as director of the Agricultural Experiment Station. Although Kerr had been a polygamist, he divorced his second wife in 1898, eight years after the Woodruff Manifesto began the end of authorized plural marriage in the church. In the emotional upheaval that followed, both Kerr and his wives left the church.[34]

Widtsoe concluded that his appointment as experiment station director was "all right." He loved the experimentation "for which the station stood" and had prepared himself "to dedicate my life to it."[35]

---

34. Widtsoe, *Sunlit Land*, 70–71.
35. Widtsoe, *Sunlit Land*, 71.

CHAPTER FOUR

AGRICULTURAL EXPERIMENT
STATION DIRECTOR

John Widtsoe assumed the directorship of the Utah State Agricultural Experiment Station in September 1900 at about the same time that William J. Kerr became president of USAC. As he assumed the directorship, Widtsoe based his philosophy of life on the proposition that "people must live together in communities drawing their sustenance from nearby lands." Considering other occupations, he argued that "a commonwealth cannot rest upon mining or manufacturing alone." He believed that "these activities [mining and manufacturing] prosper best in the wake of agriculture," or as Daniel Webster asserted, "When tillage begins, other arts follow."[1]

In the eleven years before Widtsoe assumed the station's directorship, the station had operated entirely on meager congressional appropriations. Although Widtsoe managed to receive some additional appropriations, funds remained limited during the five years he directed the institution. With such limited funds, Widtsoe recognized that the staff would "have to choose problems for investigation of first importance in Utah." He believed that since each state had an agricultural experiment station, USAC's station should not duplicate the research conducted elsewhere. Thus, to the degree that Utahns could apply previously completed research to the state's condition, the station under Widtsoe's directorship should not replicate it.[2]

Widtsoe understood that in Utah's arid or semi-arid climate "only

---

1. John A. Widtsoe, *In a Sunlit Land: The Autobiography of John A. Widtsoe* (Salt Lake City: Milton R. Hunter and G. Homer Durham, 1952), 73.
2. Widtsoe, *Sunlit Land*, 73.

a small proportion of the desert could be irrigated even under the most favorable conditions, with water flowing from the mountains." Widtsoe also understood that, in order to determine the needs of plants, scientists would have to understand "the relationship between plants and water, historically and experimentally." At the outset, the station's staff "did not really realize that we were entering one of the least considered subjects in modern agriculture." Widtsoe called on the combined forces of "the departments of irrigation engineering, agronomy, and chemistry" to conduct the research on irrigation.[3]

In order to control the volume of water supplied to the soil, researchers in 1901 established a system of troughs and flumes that allowed them to measure the amount of water delivered "to a series of plats planted to various crops." Later the college acquired an additional farm and a vegetation house with movable tanks that they could protect from natural rainfall. They filled the tanks "with various soils" to which they delivered measurable quantities of water. Widtsoe said that "the farm and the vegetation house were undoubtedly the first experimental plant of its kind in the world dedicated to the scientific study of the use of water in irrigation." The experiment proved, in his words, "very effective."[4]

With the system he and his colleagues devised, they measured "the movement of water in irrigated soils," controlled the "loss of soil moisture by seepage and evaporation," determined "the relation between the water lost by evaporation from soils and by transpiration from plants," and found "the relation between soil fertility and plant transpiration." Their research allowed them to calculate "the actual quantities of water required" to produce crops; "the yields of crops and their chemical composition under varying quantities and times of irrigation"; and resolve other irrigation problems.[5]

Most important, this research answered three problems that demonstrated the superiority of irrigated agriculture over humid agriculture. First, by irrigating crops, they were able to control "crop quantity and quality," something humid agriculture with natural precipitation could not do. With irrigation, they could "determine ... the

3. Widtsoe, *Sunlit Land*, 74.
4. Widtsoe, *Sunlit Land*, 75.
5. Widtsoe, *Sunlit Land*, 75.

proportion of the various plant parts, and the chemical composition of the crops produced." Second, by controlling the economical use of available water, they could let farmers know how to expand the "irrigated area." This meant that by controlling the economical use of water, farmers could "meet the needs of the market," while at the same time "increase the yield and extend the area of his farm that may be irrigated." Third, by controlling the amount of water delivered to the soil, farmers could avoid "the injury to soils and plants by the excessive use of water in irrigation—the curse of irrigated sections everywhere."[6]

Because of the results of the USAC Experiment Station's experiments under Widtsoe's direction, the station received additional funding, and in addition to the college farms, they used part of the funds to expand their research to farms elsewhere in Utah. Recognizing the importance of the station's findings, the US Office of Irrigation Investigation "contributed funds" for cooperative work under Widtsoe's direction. To assist farmers in applying their research, the experiment station officers published summaries in "brief bulletins" that they distributed "widely."[7]

In addition to studying irrigated farming, Widtsoe initiated research on what scientists and practitioners called dry farming—farming without irrigation in a dry-summer Mediterranean climate. Although Utah as a whole had an average precipitation of twelve inches per year, precipitation in the farmable valleys ranged from 16.5 inches in the Salt Lake Valley to five inches in southeastern Utah's Moab.[8] Widtsoe did not claim credit for originating dry farming. Some in Utah and elsewhere had already grown crops, especially wheat, "on small areas without irrigation." He knew that if farmers could conserve moisture in the soil "by proper soil treatment," they could "produce fair crops of wheat, about fifteen bushels per acre."[9]

To investigate such farms in Utah, Widtsoe and colleague Lewis A. Merrill, a professor of agricultural engineering, set out in a white top wagon with augers and various "tools and instruments, to learn

6. Widtsoe, *Sunlit Land*, 75–76.

7. Widtsoe, *Sunlit Land*, 75–76.

8. For an overview of these conditions, see Richard H. Jackson, "Utah's Harsh Lands: Hearth of Greatness," *Utah Historical Quarterly* 49 (Winter 1981): 4–25.

9. Widtsoe, *Sunlit Land*, 76–77.

the secrets of dry farming from those who had practiced it successfully though on a small scale." To the information gleaned from such
previous dry farms, Widtsoe and Merrill "added the experimental
results from the College farm and vegetation house."[10]

Widtsoe and Merrill published the results of their research in
the deservedly famous Utah State Experiment Station "Bulletin No.
75." In it, they poked holes in some of the widely held perceptions
of the ability of soil to hold water. They, in addition to providing
information on how to do dry farming, showed from the analysis of
the subsurface in loam soil "near Collinston, Box Elder County" that
"in the first ten feet of ... [loam, the soil held] 14.27 inches [of wa-
ter], or a year's rainfall." Some people had insisted that the retention
of water had resulted from cultivation of the ground. By examin-
ing sample auger bores on an uncultivated plot near the dry farm,
Widtsoe and Merrill demonstrated that although soil cultivation
increased the moisture content of the soil to a small degree, most of
the water resulted from precipitation and not from cultivation. Their
research demonstrated that uncultivated soils held a water content
only slightly smaller than that held by nearby cultivated soils on
which farmers were growing dry farm wheat.[11]

In order to determine the suitability of a particular piece of
ground for dry farming, Widtsoe and Merrill recommended that
farmers obtain a bore sample by running an augur ten feet deep into
the soil to determine the water content at each foot of depth.[12]

Widtsoe and Merrill noted that several people had theorized on
why the soil retained so much water. Some of the water, especially on
mountainsides, resulted from seepage, but on farms lying on lower
land, the water came almost entirely from precipitation directly on
the soil. Moreover, their research showed that although most people
did not know it, "a great portion of Utah lands not yet under irrigation systems, are underlaid by water."[13]

---

10. Widtsoe, *Sunlit Land*, 77.

11. John A. Widtsoe and Lewis A. Merrill, "Bulletin No. 75—Arid Framing or
Dry Farming," in *Utah Agricultural Extension Service Bulletins* (1902), 88–89. Hereafter
"Bulletin No. 75," with pages. See the discussion together with the results shown on
Table 7, p. 89.

12. Widtsoe and Merrill, "Bulletin No. 75," 92–93.

13. "Bulletin No. 75," 90.

Some observers believed that clayey soil offered a better venue for crops than sandy soil or loam. A problem with this point of view, Widtsoe pointed out, is that research had shown that soil retains water as a film around soil particles. This means that clayey soil holds more water, but only because the soil particles are smaller than loam which has larger particles and sand in which the particles are even larger. Clay might hold more water, but because the water is dispersed around minuscule particles, less water is available for plants to use.[14]

Widtsoe and Merrill tried to determine in which sections of Utah farmers could successfully grow crops by dry farming. They knew that such farming could succeed on the Wasatch Front, in Cache Valley, and in some parts of Juab and Tooele Counties because farmers had dry-farmed there. In other areas of the state they were unsure because farmers had not tried it. Nevertheless, they speculated that dry farming could succeed in some other areas. To make water available to crops, they recommended deep plowing to free the available moisture in the soil. In addition, they recommended fall rather than spring planting despite the possibility that in a year with minimal snowfall some of the crop might winter-kill. The authors suggested that the farmers consider fallowing the land, but only under certain conditions. Farmers, they said, needed to understand the character of their land before determining whether to fallow every second year, every third year, or not at all and whether to plant a crop such as clover during the fallow season in order to restore fertility of the land, especially to enhance its nitrogen content.[15] They recommended that farmers successfully engage in dry farming if their field had deep soil and the farm lay in a region with annual precipitation of more than ten inches. In order to test their research in actual conditions throughout the state, the legislature and Governor Heber M. Wells authorized the experiment station to establish nine exploratory farms in various areas of the state.[16]

After Widtsoe proposed to establish one of the farms on the mountain near Levan, he met with the Juab County commissioners to obtain their cooperation. The commissioners proposed to put the

---

14. "Bulletin No. 75," 92.
15. "Bulletin No. 75," 96–97, 100–109, 111–12.
16. Widtsoe, *Sunlit Land*, 77.

farm on a south-facing slope, but Widtsoe located it on a north-facing slope. When Widtsoe and his colleagues succeeded in growing a crop, one critic thought at first they had fortunately located the only north-facing slope in the area on which wheat would grow. Later, after considering the matter, he concluded that Widtsoe had been right, and even succeeded himself, in farming on a north-facing slope near Levan. Following Widtsoe's experiment, farmers covered the slopes near Levan with "thousands of acres of grain and useful crops." Some of the farmers succeeded in growing an astounding fifty bushels of wheat per acre instead of the anticipated fifteen bushels.[17]

Interest in expanding dry farming because of the research of Widtsoe and Merrill spread throughout Utah and the rest of the world. Because "two-thirds of the earth's land surface lies under low rainfall," Widtsoe concluded, "the whole world was interested." Requests for "Bulletin No. 75" came from nation after nation, and people throughout the world came to Logan to gain more information on dry farming. Dry farming in Utah, Idaho, and other dry-summer states increased from a few thousand acres to "hundreds of thousands or millions of acres."[18]

Although the station's research in irrigation and dry farming received most of the public attention, scientists there conducted experiments in other areas as well. Some of these included soil surveys, alkali land reclamation, feed value of crops, and expansion of the livestock industry.[19]

Although Widtsoe and his colleagues understood that their studies could improve farming practices and make it more profitable for Utah's farmers, they encountered considerable conservatism and prejudice against what opponents called "book farmers." In the face of such opposition, Widtsoe and his colleagues understood that their experiments and bulletins could do little good if they could not successfully disseminate information to those who actually tilled and planted the soil.[20]

---

17. Widtsoe, *Sunlit Land*, 80; Reuben B. Young et al., Affidavit, Apr. 18, 1918, inserted between pp. 80–81.

18. Widtsoe, *Sunlit Land*, 77–78.

19. Widtsoe, *Sunlit Land*, 78.

20. Widtsoe, *Sunlit Land*, 78–79.

Widtsoe and colleagues selected a two-pronged approach to break down the prejudice and circulate the knowledge they had acquired. They fashioned one prong out of literature. J. Edward Taylor, Merrill, and Widtsoe began the publication of a weekly magazine, *The Deseret Farmer*. The title sought to capture attention of Utah's predominantly LDS agricultural population by using both the Book of Mormon word *Deseret* and the occupational word *Farmer* in the title. Later publishers changed the name to *The Utah Farmer*, but the first effort to link the title to the LDS tradition helped to get it into the homes and fields of many Utah farmers. From his experience with the publication, Widtsoe concluded that it had "done much to help the tiller of the soil and the husbandman in the arid region."[21] In a second prong, Widtsoe, E. D. Ball, and others held institutes in various counties to disseminate information directly in gatherings of farmers.[22]

As Widtsoe continued his research at the experiment station, he also engaged in other activities and in managing a home. He became a lobbyist for the college and experiment station, and in that capacity, he learned how politics worked on the grassroots level. When he saw what actually happened, he became somewhat critical of the way in which partisan party discipline undermined the effort to meet constituent needs. He realized that legislators often voted with their party rather than do what was best for the people in their districts.

He also contributed time and money to promote the interests of the college and experiment station. He served on a number of state boards to promote the interests of the college. During Widtsoe's years at the experiment station, the state paid educators very poorly, and he and Leah had to live quite frugally. Nevertheless, as director of the experiment station, he drew on those meager resources to host dinners at his home for visitors from the United States, Europe, and Asia.[23]

In addition to his professional activity, he devoted considerable time and effort to support the religion to which he had converted. He traveled frequently in a professional capacity, but he also worked actively in his local ward seventies quorum and served on his

---

21. Widtsoe, *Sunlit Land*, 79.
22. Widtsoe, *Sunlit Land*, 79.
23. Widtsoe, *Sunlit Land*, 82.

local stake Sunday school board. He served for a couple of years as president of the Fifth Ward Young Men's Mutual Improvement Association (YMMIA). Leah served concurrently as president of the Young Women's Mutual Improvement Association (YWMIA). In 1905 church leaders called him as a member of the churchwide general board of the YMMIA, which required his frequent travel to Salt Lake City. As an added benefit, however, he became well acquainted with LDS Church President Joseph F. Smith who served not only as prophet but also as general superintendent of the MIA. B. H. Roberts, one of the Seven Presidents of the Seventy, served as Smith's second counselor and Heber J. Grant, an apostle who succeeded Smith as church president, served as Smith's first counselor.[24]

Putting his literary talents to use, Widtsoe also began writing manuals and other works for the church. These included study outlines for the Sunday school on the Doctrine and Covenants and the Old Testament, and lesson outlines for the MIA. He also published a number of articles in churchwide general interest *The Improvement Era*, a monthly magazine. It is unclear how he found time to do the intensive research necessary for such a work, but he also published the book-length *Concordance of the Doctrine and Covenants*. During this period, he was perhaps best known for his book *Joseph Smith as Scientist* that was first published in part as a series of articles in the *Improvement Era*. The book compared Joseph Smith's philosophy with pre-Einsteinian science. It served as a study course for the YMMIA.[25]

During debates on the Utah State Constitution in 1895, a number of delegates favored consolidation of the University of Utah and USAC. Unswayed by their arguments, the majority of convention delegates voted to continue to support two institutions and wrote that provision into the state constitution.

That did not, however, settle the question, nor did it definitively define the educational scope of the two institutions. Agricultural College President W. J. Kerr, who proposed a very expansive mission for the college in Logan, mapped "out a very comprehensive

---

24. Widtsoe, *Sunlit Land*, 83.

25. Widtsoe, *Sunlit Land*, 83; Thomas G. Alexander, *Mormonism in Transition: A History of the Latter-day Saints, 1890–1930* (3rd ed.; Salt Lake City: Greg Kofford Books, 2012), 291.

field for college operations." In addition to agricultural education and classes in those subjects necessary for a well-rounded graduate such as literature, English, and history, Kerr proposed to add schools of engineering and mining. In college faculty meetings Widtsoe forcefully opposed this expansion as "unnecessary duplication" with the mission of the University of Utah. Unlike agricultural engineer Lewis Merrill, however, Widtsoe did not speak out publicly on his views. Nevertheless, Merrill published an article in the *Deseret Farmer* arguing that "agriculture in the State was really endangered," most likely by Kerr's proposed expansion. He insisted that Kerr's proposal departed "from the true mission of the College." Angry, Kerr apparently assumed that Widtsoe had been involved in public opposition to his plans, and in June 1905 he dismissed Widtsoe from the experiment station and the faculty.[26]

Widtsoe understood that he could probably find a position in his field outside Utah, but Kerr's dismissal in June presented an obstacle. Widtsoe knew that most institutions of higher learning had already filled their faculty and research positions during the spring—certainly by May. Relying on the avenues at hand, Widtsoe knew he had friends within the church leadership, and he "took counsel with those I trusted best." Recognizing the unusual opportunity to hire a PhD chemist who had made an exceptional reputation as director of the USAC Experiment Station, LDS-owned Brigham Young University offered him a faculty position, and he and Leah relocated their family 105 miles south to Provo.[27]

The move to Provo occurred out of necessity during difficult circumstances. It had not occurred, however, because Widtsoe had failed as director of the USAC Experiment Station. During his five years in Logan, Widtsoe had revolutionized two fields of farming. Through experiments with irrigated agriculture and the dissemination of information, Widtsoe, Merrill, and their staff had demonstrated that with the economical application of irrigation water on Utah's fields, farmers could expand their cultivated crops while avoiding the destruction of their land by overwatering. Using

26. Widtsoe, *Sunlit Land*, 84–86.
27. Widtsoe, *Sunlit Land*, 87.

Widtsoe's expertise in organic chemistry, they showed the proper techniques to produce healthy crops for the market.

Perhaps the field in which Widtsoe's work is best known, however, was in the dissemination of information on the most effective methods of dry farming. Widtsoe and Merrill showed that in areas with deep soil and precipitation of more than ten inches per year Utah's lands could produce healthy and nutritious wheat crops ranging from fifteen to fifty bushels per acre. Their studies with an augur demonstrated that such lands contained enough water for an annual crop, especially with deep plowing and fall planting.

Significantly, Widtsoe and Merrill succeeded in disseminating the results of their research throughout the world. "Bulletin No. 75" of the Experiment Station became a bible for those whose lands received too little precipitation during the growing season. Widtsoe became a hero to agricultural communities throughout the world.

CHAPTER FIVE

THE ACADEMIC IMPROVEMENT OF BRIGHAM YOUNG UNIVERSITY

Brigham Young, second president of the LDS Church, endowed three institutions that he expected to grow into citadels of higher learning. Latter-day Saint University (LDSU) in Salt Lake City and Brigham Young College (BYC) in Logan tried unsuccessfully to compete with the University of Utah and USAC. For a time, LDSU survived as the LDS Business College (renamed Ensign College in 2020) and as the McCune School of Music and Art which offered instruction in the McCune Mansion on North Main Street in Salt Lake City from 1922 until 1957. BYC operated as a high school with some collegiate instruction from 1877 to 1926 when the college shut down and the Logan School District acquired its property.

Founded in 1875 as Brigham Young Academy, Brigham Young University at first functioned basically as an elementary school and high school. After its beginning under the presidency of Warren N. Dusenberry, BYA came under the leadership of Karl G. Maeser. Educated at a teacher's school and seminar in Dresden, Saxony, Maeser taught in Dresden until his conversion and baptism in the LDS Church. He was generally called Dr. Maeser, but he obtained an honorary doctorate from the Church Board of Education. He had to leave Dresden after joining the church because Germany refused to permit the church to exist there. Maeser served as BYA president until 1892 when he resigned to become Superintendent of Church Schools.

Maeser's influence and ideas affected BYA even after his death in 1901. He believed in the importance of linking religious and secular education, and BYU had continued in that tradition when Widtsoe joined the faculty in 1905. The academy had already shed its elementary school curriculum by 1903 when the church leadership divided it into Brigham Young High School and Brigham Young University. Like both USAC and the University of Utah in 1905 when Widtsoe joined the faculty, BYU "was emerging from a high school-college condition." The university enrolled ninety college students during the 1905 to 1906 school year.[1] George H. Brimhall, then university president, had no advanced education, but like Maeser, he received an honorary doctorate from the Church Board of Education.[2] Other teachers, whom Widtsoe considered "good teachers, better far than the average," but without advanced degrees were Nels L. Nelson (English and Spanish) and Joseph B. Keeler (theology, accounting, and administration).[3] By contrast, Edwin S. Hinckley (geology and education), whom Widtsoe considered "better far than the average," had studied at the University of Michigan after graduating from Brigham Young Academy.[4] Others who studied at distinguished institutions of higher learning and who served on the BYU faculty during Widtsoe's tenure there included Josiah H. Hickman (psychology), James L. Brown (elementary education), Alice Louise Reynolds (English), John C. Swenson (economics and sociology), and Harvey Fletcher (physics and mathematics).[5]

After USAC President Kerr fired Widtsoe in the summer of 1905, George Brimhall was so anxious to hire Widtsoe at BYU that he secured "a special appropriation from the Church Board of Education to cover Widtsoe's salary of $2,200.[6]

Brimhall brought Widtsoe to Provo to organize an agriculture department. At Widtsoe's recommendation, he also secured the

---

1. Ernest L. Wilkinson and W. Cleon Skousen, *Brigham Young University: A School of Destiny* (Provo, UT: Brigham Young University Press, 1976), 189.

2. John A. Widtsoe, *In a Sunlit Land: The Autobiography of John A. Widtsoe* (Salt Lake City: Milton R. Hunter and G. Homer Durham, 1952), 91.

3. Davis Bitton, "N. L. Nelson and The Mormon Point of View," *BYU Studies* 13, no. 2 (1973): 153–71.

4. Wilkinson and Skousen, *Brigham Young University*, 181.

5. Wilkinson and Skousen, *Brigham Young University*, 185; Ernest L. Wilkinson, ed., *Brigham Young University: The First One Hundred Years*, Vol. 1 (Provo, UT: Brigham Young University Press, 1975): 579–90.

6. Wilkinson and Skousen, *Brigham Young University* (1976), 184.

part-time assistance of Lewis A. Merrill and William H. Homer Jr. Merrill was an agricultural engineer who had worked with Widtsoe on his irrigation and dry farming research; Homer was an outstanding horticulturalist.[7]

Widtsoe envisioned the BYU agriculture department in the broadest terms. He encouraged students to enroll in the department, and because of his reputation as a research chemist and teacher, the "classes grew in numbers." Reaching out to the agricultural public, he also organized lectures to help farmers around the state improve their agricultural practices. On weekends, Widtsoe organized farmers' institutes in which Leah also participated by offering classes to farmers' wives on home economics.[8]

While on the BYU faculty, Widtsoe continued research that he had begun before moving to BYU. In 1903, Widtsoe and Merrill had begun an investigation of the affects of smelter smoke on plants and animals. In 1903 it had become apparent that a series of smelters built in the years before had caused damage to crops and animals. In 1899 the Utah Consolidated Gold Mines, Ltd., operated by Samuel Newhouse and Thomas Weir, completed construction of two smelters in the Salt Lake Valley to process copper and lead ores. In 1900 Edward L. White, W. S. McCornick, and Duncan McVichie began operating a "semipyritic" smelter also in the Salt Lake Valley, and the United States mining Company under Albert E. Holden began construction of a 1,000 ton capacity copper smelter at Bingham Junction.[9]

Before 1903 the smelters apparently had no perceptible effect on Salt Lake Valley farms. During the summer of 1903, however, severe wind and rain spread smelter smoke which devastated a strip of land in Salt Lake County from Murray to Salt Lake City. Because of the apparent damage, in June 1903 Widtsoe and Merrill began their research on the Salt Lake County area. Widtsoe's research confirmed what farmers knew from experience. Smelter smoke contained sulphur dioxide that, when mixed with water,

7. Widtsoe, *Sunlit Land*, 92.

8. Widtsoe, *Sunlit Land*, 92–93.

9. John E. Lamborn and Charles S. Peterson, "The Substance of the Land: Agriculture v. Industry in the Smelter Cases of 1904 and 1906," *Utah Historical Quarterly* 53 (Fall 1985): 312.

generated sulphuric acid that poisoned crops and animals. His research showed as well that smoke from the smelters carried "into the very heart of Salt Lake City."[10]

A problem Widtsoe faced in his study resulted from the capricious nature of the wind and rain. Rainfall combined with dust clouds and downdrafts during irrigation exacerbated the smoke damage. The research of Widtsoe's team showed that when "wind causes the smoke to beat upon a field for a considerable length of time, it tends to injure the crops severely ... [and] it tends to injure animals that are ... in [the] line of the prevailing winds." "Flue dust" carried by "washing of rains and melting snows ... may occasionally poison pools of standing water."[11]

On the positive side, Widtsoe's chemical analysis showed that the smoke did not "injure the fertility of the soils nor materially affect the feeding value of crops grown in the area." More seriously, however, Widtsoe suggested certain precautions to prevent damage to plants and animals that he considered "practical," but which proved difficult to apply. These included not irrigating when winds blow "smoke towards your farm"; growing hay "on the affected pastures"; feeding animals in the barn as much as possible; not "plant[ing] orchards or trees of any kind in the districts affected by smelter smoke"; observing that lucern "appears to withstand the effect of the smelter smoke very well"; and planting windbreaks to shelter "a farm from the direct action of the smoke." As an addendum, Widtsoe suggested that misfortunes might come from other causes. He urged the farmers to "be reasonable in your claims, then insist upon your rights." Widtsoe pointed that since the smelters employed a large number of people, they "afforded" a market for agricultural goods that was "of decided advantage to the farmers." At the same time, he noted that "the interests ... of the mining industry were furthered by the proximity of prosperous agricultural communities."[12]

Although Widtsoe's report detailed the causes of the smoke pollution, farmers did not appreciate his remedies. Instead of mitigating the damage by following Widtsoe's suggestions, farmers wanted the

10. Widtsoe, *Sunlit Land*, 93.
11. Lamborn and Peterson, "Substance of the Land," 313–14.
12. Lamborn and Peterson, "Substance of the Land," 312–15.

smelters to "stop the smoke altogether" or adjust "the operation of the plants."[13]

Deseret News editor Charles W. Penrose, of the Quorum of the Twelve Apostles, tried to smooth the troubled waters. He published a series of editorials between August and September in 1904 recommending at first conciliation and later arbitration.[14]

Unwilling to settle for arbitration when the smoke threatened "their lives, their homes, and their property," farmers took more active measures. In December 1904 they filed petitions with the Salt Lake County commissioners and the State Board of Health. In February 1905, farmers and smelter operators met with the Salt Lake County Board of Health. The farmers asked "that the smoke be declared a public nuisance and that steps be taken to abate it." The smelter operators wanted more time.[15]

After the boards of health did little to help them, because of the damage to their crops and animals, farmers filed several suits, but the one with the greatest impact was *James Godfrey et al.* v. *American Smelting and Refining Company et al.* In this suit, the 419 farmers who filed took on five smelters. The suit outlined the chemical process which Widtsoe's research had uncovered showing that "in the process of smelting sulphur dioxide fumes are generated and escape." The addition of moisture creates "sulphuric acid" that cools and "falls to the ground" where it injures "growing vegetation." In addition, "dust escapes from the smelter stack," injuring vegetation and livestock which eat the hay on which the dust has fallen.[16]

Following an extensive hearing, Judge John A. Marshall granted an injunction that required that the smelters process ore with no more than 10 percent sulfur content. Marshall issued a permanent injunction against smelters that failed or refused to meet that standard. All but the American Smelting and Refining Company closed or moved their operations from the Midvale-Murray area. American Smelting and Refining paid the farmers $60,000 in compensation to allow its continued operation. Other smelters found more radical

---

13. Lamborn and Peterson, "Substance of the Land," 314–15.
14. Lamborn and Peterson, "Substance of the Land," 315–16.
15. Lamborn and Peterson, "Substance of the Land," 317.
16. Lamborn and Peterson, "Substance of the Land," 319.

ways to solve their problems. The Highland Boy closed in 1907, the Utah Consolidated closed its smelter and sent its ores to the International Smelter in Tooele, the Bingham Consolidated closed its smelter in 1907, the United States Mining Company closed its smelter in 1908.[17]

Not everyone loved the farmers for purifying Salt Lake County air. Some people in Murray and Midvale lashed out at the farmers for undermining "their source of revenue." The *Salt Lake Tribune*, more favorably inclined to the mining and smelting industry than the *Deseret News*, opined that the farmers seemed like "the fabled gent who killed the goose that laid the golden eggs." Smelter operators appealed the decision to the tenth circuit court which sustained Marshall's verdict. Some smelters made the accommodations mentioned above, but others relocated to Garfield and Magna; smoke from the Magna area continued to create a problem for farms in Salt Lake Valley. Moreover, smoke from the Murray smelter continued to plague farmers well into the mid-twentieth century.[18]

During his years at BYU, Widtsoe remained active in the church. Wards and stakes frequently called upon him to talk to their meetings. He wrote several study courses for auxiliary organizations including a two-year course for the Young Women's MIA on the Doctrine and Covenants. He also continued to serve on the general board of the Young Men's MIA.

At BYU, he served as a mentor for a group of young men. He was anxious to do this because of his perception of the importance of BYU since it linked religious and secular education. The group included Franklin S. Harris, George R. Hill, R. J. Evans, and Ernest Caroll. In addition, Widtsoe understood that in order to succeed and grow, BYU had to solicit and receive financial contributions from alumni and others.[19]

Widtsoe's tenure at BYU lasted only for two years. During that time, he organized an agriculture department that began academic work in farming and other similar pursuits. His research in documenting the damage that smelter smoke did to crops and animals

---

17. Lamborn and Peterson, "Substance of the Land," 320–21.
18. Lamborn and Peterson, "Substance of the Land," 322–25.
19. Widtsoe, *Sunlit Land*, 95–97.

proved important especially for the suits farmers initiated to begin the effort to clean the air along the Wasatch Front. His service as a mentor helped several young men achieve prominence. Franklin Harris, for instance, became president of both BYU and USAC.

CHAPTER SIX

THE RETURN TO USAC

The story of Widtsoe's firing in 1905 and his rehiring in 1907 to re-place William J. Kerr as USAC president reflects not only on Kerr but also on members of the Board of Trustees. In 1905 when Kerr proposed to fire Widtsoe and Louis A. Merrill, a majority of the board of trustees led by Board President William S. McCornick sustained Kerr's recommendation. In 1907, however, Utah governor John C. Cutler reorganized the board. McCornick resigned as president in disgust, and Cutler appointed Lorenzo N. Stohl as McCornick's successor. He also appointed Thomas Smart, president of the First National Bank of Logan; John Q. Adams, a Davis County community leader; Susa Young Gates, daughter of Brigham Young, Leah's mother, and a community and LDS Church leader; and Elizabeth C. McCune, a Salt Lake City community leader, as board members.[1]

On March 28, 1907, the newly appointed board met in the office of Utah Secretary of State C. S. Tingey in Salt Lake City. The board reversed some of Kerr's actions. Kerr resigned as USAC president, at the board's insistence. In his place, they appointed Widtsoe. At the same meeting, the board removed P. A. Yoder as experiment station director and appointed E. D. Ball, an appointment Widtsoe recommended, to replace him. They also appointed Louis A. Merrill, whom Kerr had fired at the same time he fired Widtsoe, as director of extension work.[2]

Widtsoe's appointment generated considerable controversy. In 1905, a brouhaha had arisen over Kerr's initiative to add a number of

---

1. *Salt Lake Tribune*, Mar. 29, 1907.

2. *Salt Lake Tribune*, Mar. 29, 1907, John A. Widtsoe, *In a Sunlit Land: the Autobiography of John A. Widtsoe* (Salt Lake City: Milton R. Hunter and G. Homer Durham, 1952), 98–99.

collegiate departments to reorganize USAC as a competitor to the University of Utah. Kerr's initiative created opposition both because of the additional cost it would entail and the perceived downgrading of agricultural education and research. The Utah legislature refused to support Kerr's proposal, and the political fallout led to reduced appropriations for the college.[3]

After his appointment as president, Widtsoe traveled to Salt Lake City and to Logan a week before he moved his family back to Cache County. In Salt Lake City, he sought divine help by securing a blessing from Joseph F. Smith and the church's First Presidency. In Logan, he found the emotional and political climate hostile among community leaders and portions of the faculty. At least four faculty members resigned in protest over Kerr's removal. Nevertheless, although Widtsoe had an excellent relationship with the board during his nine years as college president, he understood that he had to mend fences with town and gown because he knew "when the Board assumes control of an institution its days are numbered, or its usefulness curtailed."[4]

Widtsoe intended to emphasize those subjects for which the Morrill Act had authorized the agricultural college's establishment and for which Congress designated the selection of lands in the Morrill Act and the Utah State Enabling Act of 1894. As Widtsoe wrote, "Its mission was to dignify and make more successful farming, mechanic arts, home economics, and commerce, the pursuits of ordinary men and women." Significantly, Widtsoe did not qualify his perception by mentioning that the "ordinary men and women" were rural rather than urban.[5]

In addition to emphasizing farming, mechanic arts, home economics, and commerce, Widtsoe understood that the college must also offer "classes [in] the general cultural subjects which every citizen should know for his own happiness." These included such subjects as English, literature, history, and physical education. He thought these

---

3. Widtsoe, *Sunlit Land*, 98–99, 101. At the time Utah's legislature met only every two years so appropriations had to suffice for the biennium.

4. Widtsoe, *Sunlit Land*, 99–100; *Salt Lake Tribune*, Mar. 29, 1907.

5. Widtsoe, *Sunlit Land*, 100.

additions were necessary because, in his view, "a practical and a liberal education should be welded into one for the use of the many."[6]

The controversy over the consolidation of the University of Utah and USAC again came before the legislature in its biennial session in 1907. Consolidation failed by a minuscule majority. Instead of simply leaving the two institutions separate, however, the legislature passed a bill restricting USAC operations to the subjects listed in the Morrill Act and previous Utah legislation. The law prohibited USAC from offering courses in engineering. In an additional slap, however, in 1907, the legislature, which met only every two years at the time, reduced appropriations for its operation for the next biennium at "a smaller sum than usual."[7]

Although Widtsoe had assumed the agricultural college's presidency as a result of a controversy over the college's academic mission, he was inclined to try to promote peace and shun conflict. Through strenuous effort, he made friends with the minority members of the Board of Trustees. In addition, in an effort to save the college from disaster, he spent "many years of lobbying," in which he experienced "a real course of instruction in American politics." Certainly his close relationship with prominent Latter-day Saints, especially the church leadership, helped him, but he had to address the interests of non-Mormons as well.[8]

Widtsoe faced an immediate problem because the Logan business community and the city's principal newspaper, the *Logan Journal,* had come down squarely on Kerr's side. As in most college towns, Logan business people valued "the institution because of the money it brings to the town." Although many in business recognized the value of a higher education, others thought principally of the monetary benefit. Since Widtsoe had grown up in Logan, however, he still retained close friendships with a number of prominent citizens including Melvin J. Ballard, Joseph E. Cardon, and Joseph Quinney Jr.[9]

Widtsoe had many problems with which he had to cope. One of the most difficult was to convert the *Logan Journal* to support

---

6. Widtsoe, *Sunlit Land,* 100–1.
7. Widtsoe, *Sunlit Land,* 101.
8. Widtsoe, *Sunlit Land,* 101.
9. Widtsoe, *Sunlit Land,* 102–3.

him. The *Journal* was a Democratic Party organ, and Kerr had been an active Democrat, Widtsoe a Republican. Unfortunately for the *Journal*, from 1907 to 1917 Utah Republicans occupied the executive and judicial seats in Utah's government, and the Republican Party had a majority in both houses of the legislature. Fortunately for Widtsoe, his administration brought success to the college and the size of the student body increased under his administration, both of which benefitted Logan's business community, and the paper's tone shifted to support him.[10]

In addition to cementing relations with business people and the *Logan Journal's* editor, he had to secure the support of the faculty. The consolidation controversy had generated "unrest" among the faculty. The faculty divided between factions of those favoring expansion of the college to compete with the University of Utah, those favoring consolidation of the two institutions, and those supporting the "original act of creation." Widtsoe managed to cement his relationship with most of the faculty, and he came to look upon many "as warm personal friends," who worked together with him to create "big things for the State of Utah." Others, he considered "congenitally disloyal." He believed that these "seldom [constructed] anything worthwhile." Rather, "they usually poison the minds of youth by their sour attitudes," and he believed "they ... should be removed."[11]

Widtsoe had to struggle with constant faculty replacement. He estimated that faculty composition turned over every three and a half years. He hoped to reduce the turnover and to promote faculty permanence. Most of the faculty came from the eastern United States. Many of these remained only until they could secure a position nearer to their hometowns or in an institution that paid a better salary. Widtsoe understood that such turnover injured "the institution."[12]

Widtsoe addressed the problem of turnover in two ways. Faculty salaries were "extremely low," especially in comparison with peer institutions, and Widtsoe lobbied for an increase. With extremely hard work, he achieved a "fixed schedule for various ranks" at "nearly twenty percent above the previous level." Nevertheless, he

---

10. Widtsoe, *Sunlit Land*, 103.
11. Widtsoe, *Sunlit Land*, 104–5.
12. Widtsoe, *Sunlit Land*, 105.

still considered the new level too low. He also secured approval from the board for a sabbatical leave program. Widtsoe discussed this program in terms of a period of rest. By contrast, most faculty members consider a sabbatical leave as a time for educational enrichment or a period to finish a book or another research project. Widtsoe lamented his failure to secure a faculty pension program, but he concluded that the "time was not ripe for retirement allowances."[13]

A second tack Widtsoe took to increase faculty longevity was to encourage people from the west, especially those who took undergraduate degrees from western universities and colleges, to obtain advanced degrees from nationally prominent institutions. He expected that many would return to faculties in Utah with a master's or doctoral degree. He made some progress in this especially at the experiment station. During his tenure as president, "the Utah State Agricultural Experiment Station numbered a larger proportion of men on its staff holding the Ph.D. degree than any other station in the country," and nearly "all of these men were from the West." Moreover, "Several of them … achieved world-wide recognition."[14]

Some critics charged that by hiring of those with advanced degrees who had earned an undergraduate degree from a Utah institution, Widtsoe encouraged "inbreeding." Widtsoe considered this "pure academic poppycock." He believed, rightly in my estimation, if they did their graduate work at another institution, they were not inbred. At such institutions potential faculty were exposed to the ideas and experience of professors at some of the best institutions in the world. Moreover, Widtsoe noted that some of the major universities employed their own graduates. From his experience as an undergraduate, he knew that Harvard, "maintained on their faculty rolls a great many of their own graduates who never have been elsewhere to study." He believed that encouraging excellent students to secure an advanced degree at a prestigious institution then hiring them at a Utah institution helped to build "a permanent, well-trained faculty."[15]

Because of the dearth of high schools in Utah during the first decade of the twentieth century, most students who entered either

---

13. Widtsoe, *Sunlit Land*, 105–6.
14. Widtsoe, *Sunlit Land*, 106.
15. Widtsoe, *Sunlit Land*, 107.

USAC or the University of Utah had to enroll in some preparatory classes. Public secondary education did not exist in Utah until the last decade of the nineteenth century and did not become a viable part of Utah's educational system until the second decade of the twentieth century. In 1910, only 58 percent of Utah's sixteen-to-seventeen-year-olds were enrolled in high school.[16] At the time Widtsoe became president of USAC in 1907, the college required students who enrolled there to have taken two years of high school. Widtsoe struggled to convince some faculty members that college students needed additional high school instruction before enrolling in college. Those who opposed his proposal feared that such a requirement would reduce student enrollment. Nevertheless, Widtsoe continued to push the matter, and in 1911 the college required three years of high school work. In 1914, the institution increased the requirement to four years, which would have constituted graduation from high school.

Widtsoe also believed that with the improvement that had taken place in the quality of USAC's faculty, the institution could offer an advanced degree. Many of the same faculty members who opposed the strengthening of the college's entrance requirements opposed the introduction of master's degrees. Nevertheless, with Widtsoe's recommendation and the support of the more advanced faculty, the board authorized the master's degree at Utah State. Although Widtsoe did not say so, ordinarily one difference between a university and a college is that the university offers advanced degrees and a college does not. He believed that the quality of those who earned the master's degree demonstrated the wisdom of introducing the advanced degree. He believed that institutions in Utah should eventually offer the doctorate and that some of the faculty would oppose that change as well. Such a step would require the hiring of "well-trained" faculty qualified to offer such advanced degrees to others. He believed that Utah's institutions would have little difficulty finding positions for those who earned such degrees.[17]

As a matter of personal philosophy, Widtsoe believed that a college should offer educational opportunities away from the Logan campus. The college continued to organize farmers' institutes in

---

16. Frederick S. Buchanan, "Education in Utah," uen.org (accessed July 19, 2021).
17. Widtsoe, *Sunlit Land*, 108–9.

various places throughout the state. Widtsoe believed that, in addition, USAC should offer help to farmers and their wives through an extension division. In 1907, the board authorized the college to organize the extension division Widtsoe had sought. Widtsoe assigned his colleague Lewis A. Merrill to begin extension work, and they chose Salt Lake City as the headquarters.

Widtsoe also expanded the work of farmers' institutes. After securing the cooperation of the railroads that passed through Utah, USAC installed exhibits and lectures on trains and sent them to those areas served by railroad lines. The Denver and Rio Grande Railroad reached into eastern and southern Utah, and the tracks of the Union Pacific reached from Cache Valley through southwestern Utah. Unfortunately, during Widtsoe's tenure, rail lines did not serve some rural communities such as Fillmore, Beaver, Cedar City, St. George, Panguitch, and Kanab.[18]

Widtsoe expressed concern that few people who lived outside Cache Valley had ever visited the campus in Logan. To try to solve that problem, he established USAC Farmers' Round Up. The college held these roundups in January when most farmers experienced a slow season on the farm. The opportunity to learn improved ways of farming excited those who attended. Many of those who attended shared the knowledge with friends who did not or could not come. The Round Up became so popular that people in southern Utah requested a similar opportunity. In response, the college established a Southern Utah Round Up at Richfield. The Richfield Round Up proved as successful as the one in Logan.[19]

The college also established what Widtsoe called a correspondence department—often called continuing education. Through this department, anyone could enroll in any class offered on campus and study the material taught in Logan in their home. Some of these correspondence classes offered college credit. To supplement and support these classes, faculty members often visited communities to "conduct classes for study groups."[20] Widtsoe also promoted the

18. Widtsoe, *Sunlit Land*, 109; Delorme Mapping, *Utah Atlas & Gazetteer* (Freeport, ME: Delorme Mapping, n.d.), passim.

19. Widtsoe, *Sunlit Land*, 109–10.

20. Widtsoe, *Sunlit Land*, 116–17.

establishment of county extension agents, and Utah was one of the first to use them. The first agent was appointed in 1911 for service in the Uintah Basin.[21] Widtsoe had a strong conviction of the immense value of such extension work and correspondence education. He believed such benefitted both student and teacher.[22] Widtsoe himself had personal experience with the life of common folks. After the death of his father, who had been a teacher and community leader, his mother had helped support the family by sewing.

Widtsoe presided over the celebration of USAC's twenty-fifth anniversary in 1913. He invited Jeremiah W. Sanborn, who had served as college president during its early years, to speak at the celebration and to receive an honorary degree. He also arranged for six farmers who had adopted advanced methods to receive a certificate designating them as "Master Farmers."[23]

John and Leah also promoted education for women. On the farm in the nineteenth and early-twentieth centuries, women generally cared for the vegetable garden, cultivated small fruits such as raspberries and strawberries, and raised chickens for eggs and meat. The farm wife prepared meals for the family and for any farm hands who worked for them, and she cared for the small children. Children old enough to do chores generally worked with their father or mother. The men generally worked in the fields and managed the larger farm animals such as cows and horses. Both men and women slopped the pigs, and both usually helped to milk the cows morning and evening.[24]

John and Leah believed that women deserved to receive an education in the best techniques to carry out their homemaker duties on the farm. Although principles of domesticity were being taught as early as the mid-nineteenth century, the term "home economics" was not applied to this area of study until the early twentieth century.[25] In order to hold classes on home economics, the two of them lobbied the legislature to provide funds to convert an old dormitory

---

21. Widtsoe, *Sunlit Land*, 114–15.

22. Widtsoe, *Sunlit Land*, 111.

23. Widtsoe, *Sunlit Land*, 114.

24. Widtsoe, *Sunlit Land*, 116–17.

25. See sites.middlebury.edu (accessed Aug. 2, 2021).

into a home economics building. This building provided facilities for such education for a time.[26]

Leah also asked Utah Senator Reed Smoot to secure federal legislation to provide funds for home economics education as well as money for the college and experiment station to do research on home economics.[27] Smoot introduced several bills which, unfortunately, did not pass. Nevertheless, Smoot supported the Purnell Bill that passed in 1924. It provided USAC an initial amount of $20,000 for research work in new phases of agriculture, home economics, and agricultural engineering. The legislation provided that the appropriation was to increase at the rate of $10,000 each year until it reached an annual sum of $60,000.[28]

Since Widtsoe, Merrill, and the experiment station staff had done the pioneering work in irrigation and dry farming, John was anxious to see that all of the previously completed research reached the public. Much of the results of research Widtsoe and others had conducted had not yet been published, so Widtsoe encouraged the experiment station to publish bulletins especially on the relationship of water, soils, and plants. In 1911 Widtsoe himself published the book *Dry Farming*.[29] The book contained additional information that supplemented the volume of material included in "Bulletin 75." Because of the international interest in dry farming, foreign governments translated *Dry Farming* into French, Spanish, and Italian, and some governments translated parts of the book into other languages.[30]

After completing the volume on dry farming, Widtsoe turned to the research he, Merrill, and the staff had previously completed on irrigated farming. Drawing on the work they had done, Widtsoe published *Principles of Irrigation Practice* with New York City-based Macmillan in 1914. That book was a welcome supplement to his book on dry farming.[31] In the book, Widtsoe gave a great deal of

26. Widtsoe, *Sunlit Land*, 116–17.

27. Widtsoe, *Sunlit Land*, 116–17.

28. *The U.A.C. Alumni Quarterly* 1 (May 1925): 6, at digitalcommons.usu.edu (accessed Aug. 2, 2021).

29. John A. Widtsoe, *Dry Farming, A System of Agriculture for Countries under a Low Rainfall* (New York City: Macmillan, 1911).

30. Widtsoe, *Sunlit Land*, 118.

31. John A. Widtsoe, *The Principles of Irrigation Practice* (New York: Macmillan, 1914).

credit to the countries of Spain, France, and Italy, and he recognized that Catholic missionaries developed "mission irrigation systems … in various parts of America, notably in California." He continued, however, to contradict himself when he wrote that "the Catholic missionaries did not succeed in establishing American irrigation on a community scale, beyond that already existing among the aborigines." In fact, they developed extensive systems of *acequia* in Santa Fe, New Mexico, which the sick party that left the Mormon Battalion would have seen there in 1846.[32] Irrigation systems existed in the Southwest and California in various Spanish and Mexican missions and pueblos as well. Widtsoe gives great credit to the Mormon pioneers for their work in developing irrigation systems, but they were not the first to do so.[33]

The value of *Principles of Irrigation Practice*, however, does not lie in Widtsoe's treatment of Mormon irrigation. Rather it is an excellent treatment because of the extensive consideration of topics including soil moisture, soil changes due to irrigation, the relation of water to plants, various types of crops under irrigation, problems caused by excessive irrigation, and methods of calculating the duty of water. He emphasized that running too much water to a piece of land or failing to remove alkali substances from the soil could render the soil injurious to plant growth.[34] Unfortunately, far too many farmers in the arid region tended to believe that if a little water was good, a great deal of water was better. As a corrective, if they used the methods that Widtsoe discussed in this book, they could successfully grow valuable crops under irrigation without ruining the land or the crops.[35]

Widtsoe's interest in dry farming led him to work with others in organizing and promoting the International Dry-Farming Congress that began in 1907. In 1912 Widtsoe presided over the conference that was held that year in Lethbridge, Alberta, Canada. At one of the congresses, he met Ali Kuli Kahn, the Persian chargé d'affaires for the United States. Along with students from around the world,

---

32. Acequia Madre, www.historicsantafe.org (accessed July 21, 2021).

33. Widtsoe, *Irrigation Practice*, 454–56.

34. On the list mentioned in the paragraph, see the table of contents. On the problem of alkali, see Widtsoe, *Irrigation Practice*, 384–402.

35. Widtsoe, *Irrigation Practice*, passim.

Persia, renamed Iran, sent students to Utah to study and work at the experiment station and the college.[36]

Widtsoe faced numerous problems in addition to antagonism from the Logan community and some faculty members. Shortly after Widtsoe took office, the district manager of the local power company came to see him. He told Widtsoe that the company would double the power rates for USAC beginning June 1, 1907. Widtsoe argued with him in vain. Instead of accepting the increased rate, however, Widtsoe immediately sent out a survey crew to locate a site on the Logan River where they could establish a hydro-electric power plant to supply the college's needs. The survey party discovered a site that day, and the next day he sent a representative to Salt Lake City to file on the site. The college representative filed on the site just fifteen minutes before the power company agent got to the state office intending to file on the same site.[37]

In addition to establishing a power station, the college erected several buildings during his years as president. He oversaw the construction of a chemistry and physics building in which he reserved laboratory space for himself. After he completed his service as president, the board of trustees named the building the Widtsoe Chemistry Building in his honor. With a nest egg donated by board member Thomas Sharp, the legislature appropriated money to construct a gymnasium named for Sharp.[38]

Because of the lengthy battle over the consolidation of USAC and the University of Utah, Widtsoe thought it necessary to meet with U of U president Joseph T. Kingsbury to discuss some problems caused by the controversy. In 1907, while defining the roles of the two institutions, the legislature had prohibited Utah State from teaching engineering. Widtsoe knew that without training in the subject it would be impossible for irrigation engineers to design irrigation and machinery works. He explained these problems to Kingsbury and to Dean Joseph F. Merrill of the U's School of Mines and Engineering. The two U of U officials agreed that USAC should offer courses in agricultural engineering. As a result, Kingsbury,

---

36. Widtsoe, *Sunlit Land*, 119.
37. Widtsoe, *Sunlit Land*, 119–20.
38. Widtsoe, *Sunlit Land*, 120 and photograph inset between 120 and 121.

Merrill, and Widtsoe induced the legislature to amend the 1907 law to permit Utah State to "teach such engineering as comported with the ... mission of the College." After the passage of the legislation, Utah State organized the School of Agricultural Engineering.[39]

While serving as college president, Widtsoe also engaged in public service. In Utah he served on the state board of education and several commissions including one charged with investigating Utah's resources and making recommendations for their development. Nationally, he attended meetings of the presidents of land-grant colleges and of the National Education Association. He served for a year as vice president of the NEA. He also visited a number of land grant colleges to compare their activities, research, and teaching with those at Utah State.[40]

These activities led Widtsoe, a man who tended to reflect and think deeply, to wonder about the role of the Intermountain West in the future of the nation. He knew that the region contained some of the driest lands in America, and he wondered how they might "be put to more profitable use." Fearing that "an unoccupied strip between [the Midwest and West Coast] would endanger the future of the nation." he wondered if students "for whom I was partly responsible" might discover or invent means to facilitate the settlement and development of the region.[41]

Widtsoe thought frequently about the role of USAC in higher education. Occasionally he responded to critics who questioned the curriculum, complaining that "it did not educate students in the 'classics' or did not give them 'culture.' He gave some talks on that subject and on other themes, which friends collected in a book *Education for Necessary Pursuits*.[42]

He also continued to write for and serve in his church. His writings included study courses for the Mutual Improvement Association and other church auxiliaries and articles for the *Improvement Era*.[43] He taught "the advanced theology class," in the Logan Fifth Ward Sunday school, served on the seven-man presidency and as

---

39. Widtsoe, *Sunlit Land*, 121.
40. Widtsoe, *Sunlit Land*, 122.
41. Widtsoe, *Sunlit Land*, 122.
42. Widtsoe, *Sunlit Land*, 123.
43. Widtsoe, *Sunlit Land*, 123.

class leader of the 64th Quorum of the Seventy. After the organization of the 178th Quorum of the Seventy, he served as senior president. He was also a member of the church's general board of the Young Men's Mutual Improvement Association.[44]

Widtsoe had a firm belief that far from contradicting each other, religion and science reinforced one another. Occasionally, he found an opportunity to express a link with other scientists who shared a belief in God. In the April 1908 *Improvement Era*, he wrote a tribute to William Thompson, Lord Kelvin, who had died on December 17, 1907. Because of his scientific work in thermodynamics, scientists gave the name Kelvin to the base unit of temperature. Kelvin's life, Widtsoe pointed out, "was singularly the ideal life of the searcher for scientific truth." Widtsoe took pains to emphasize Kelvin's unwavering belief in God and his firm conviction that life continued after death. Widtsoe believed that Kelvin had "refuted many of the modern theories which teach the origin of life on this earth without the intervention of an overruling Providence." Widtsoe quoted a paragraph from Kelvin's writings: "Dead matter cannot become living without coming under the influence of matter previously alive." Kelvin believed that living matter reached earth on a celestial object such as a meteor. Widtsoe wrote:

> Carefully read, this paragraph will be found to teach that life is eternal; that life on this earth came from other spheres; that the law of natural selection is imperfect, and does not account for the variety of living things; that the law of evolution is true only as it conforms to the law of progression; that the whole of nature teaches the existence of a great designer or great governing power; and that finally, the power of free agency encircles our lives.[45]

Widtsoe, then, insisted on the need for God to begin the process of creation. "How, then, did life originate on the earth?" Widtsoe asked rhetorically. He answered, "Tracing the physical history of the earth backwards, on strict dynamical principles, we are brought to a red-hot melted globe on which no life could exist. Hence, when the earth was first fit for life, there was no living thing on it."[46]

---

44. Widtsoe, *Sunlit Land*, 124.
45. John A. Widtsoe, "Lord Kelvin, the God-Fearing," *Improvement Era* 11 (Apr. 1908): 401–3.
46. Widtsoe, "Lord Kelvin," 404.

Widtsoe turned to Darwin's *Origin of Species* for support of his belief in divine intervention in the creation of life on earth. Darwin wrote:

> It is interesting to contemplate an entangled bank clothed with many plants of many kinds, with birds singing on the bushes, with various insects flitting about, and with worms crawling through the damp earth, and to reflect that these elaborately constructed forms, so different from each other, and dependent on each other in so complex a manner, have all been produced by laws acting around us. ... There is grandeur in this view of life with its several powers having been originally breathed by the Creator into a few forms or into ones; and that, whilst this planet has gone cycling on according to the fixed law of gravity, from so simple a beginning, endless forms, most beautiful and most wonderful, have been and are being evolved."

Widtsoe wrote that with this sentiment "I must cordially sympathize." In a peroration, Widtsoe ended his tribute to Kelvin with the words: "Let us learn from the great minds of the world that in or out of this Church, there can be nothing better than a simple faith in God, and in his intelligent power over men."[47]

Widtsoe wrote the tribute to Kelvin in 1908 while he was also writing the first of two works that argued for the congruity of science and religion and the relationship of life on Earth, human life, and God. In the first book, *Joseph Smith as Scientist,* Widtsoe differentiated between natural selection and evolution. He relied more on some aspects of the views of Herbert Spencer than those of Darwin. Widtsoe agreed with Spencer that all things are in ceaseless change toward a state of increasing complexity. Widtsoe believed that instead of relying on natural selection, the increasing complexity resulted from the action of the Holy Spirit.[48]

Widtsoe argued that the Spencerian doctrine of evolution toward increasing complexity did not necessarily presuppose natural selection. He suggested an alternative view he called "the moderate law of evolution" which included an evolving God and the development of humans toward godhood. Widtsoe believed that lower animals and

---

47. Widtsoe, "Lord Kelvin," 405–6.
48. John A. Widtsoe, *Joseph Smith as Scientist: A Contribution to Mormon Philosophy* (Salt Lake City: General Board of the YMMIA, 1908), 11, 17, 19–29, 35–37, 57–60, 104–06, 113.

plants evolved just as mankind had done. He argued that animals and plants could not jump from order to order, but he admitted that the "limits of these orders are yet to be found."[49] In essence Widtsoe took a position between rejection and full acceptance of natural selection. As a PhD chemist with a specialty in organic chemistry, Widtsoe understood the classification of plants and animals. He selected "orders" as the beginning point of evolution knowing that he left considerable room for natural selection from that point. For example, scientists classify modern human beings as follows: Kingdom: Animalia, Phylum: Vertebrata, Class: Mammalia, Order: Primates, Family: Hominidae, Genus: Homo, Species: Sapiens. Clearly, both human beings and apes belong to the same order: Primates. Thus in this classification both could have evolved from a common ancestor. They belong, however, to a different family, genus, and species.

Some who read Widtsoe's book criticized him for insisting that the earth was extremely old. Some Latter-day Saints still clung tenaciously to Irish Bishop James Ussher's chronology which dated the age of the earth at about 6,000 years. After publishing his book, Widtsoe replied to those who accepted Ussher's chronology in collaboration with *Improvement Era* editor Edward H. Anderson. They wrote that the term "Day" in the Mosaic account did not mean a specific period of twenty-four hours. Bishop Ussher, himself, had abandoned the twenty-four-hour concept by arguing that a day meant 1,000 years. Widtsoe rejected even Ussher's definition of day, arguing that a day in the biblical account was an indefinite period of time. Widtsoe believed that the term day might mean "hundreds of thousands or even millions of years." He insisted also that God had created the earth in a natural way rather than bringing together fragments of other worlds.[50]

Others criticized him for believing that the luminiferous ether was the Holy Spirit. In the nineteenth century, since scientists believed that light was waves and since they knew that waves had to move through some medium, they said that the vacuum between objects in the universe was actually filled with a substance they called

49. Widtsoe, *Joseph Smith as Scientist*, 109–13.

50. Edward H. Anderson and John A. Widtsoe, "Age of the Earth, and the Time Length of Creation," *Improvement Era* 12 (Apr. 1909): 489–94.

the luminiferous ether. Widtsoe backtracked a bit by writing that both the ether and spirit were included "in the works of God." He, nevertheless, reiterated his view that Joseph Smith had discovered the "fundamental doctrine" that scientists had "been compelled by their discoveries to include in their man-made philosophy."[51]

At the time Widtsoe published his book, however, physicists had begun the research that would lead them to reject the concept of "luminiferous ether." As early as 1887, experiments on the movement of the earth and light by Albert A. Michelson and Edward W. Morley questioned the existence of the ether. Between 1900 and the 1920s physicists such as Max Planck, Albert Einstein, Niels Bohr, Werner Heisenberg, and Erwin Schrödinger discovered and elaborated quantum theory and quantum mechanics that explained that light waves moved as particles, which made the supposed luminiferous ether unnecessary. Thus, Widtsoe's views on the relationship between the luminiferous ether and the spirit of God are now outdated. In spite of these problems, *Joseph Smith as Scientist* remains in print today.

Widtsoe spent considerable time reflecting on the relationship of the church and the gospel on one hand and secular education on the other while he served as president of USAC. In addition to publishing *Joseph Smith as Scientist* in 1908, he published *A Rational Theology* in 1915. Beginning with his belief that all truth harmonizes, Widtsoe had an easier time in reconciling the creation of the universe and the earth with science than traditional Catholic and Protestant theologians who believed in creation *ex nihilo*—that God created the universe out of nothing.

Widtsoe argued that the universe was eternal. God did not create it; he organized it from preexisting matter. Widtsoe's view is compatible with both the Big Bang Theory and the steady state theory, although its compatibility with the steady state theory would depend on matter being created from something including energy rather than from nothing. The Big Bang Theory holds that the universe began as a "primeval atom" that contained the substances that later expanded into all matter. The steady state theory posits that the density of matter in the

---

51. John A. Widtsoe, "Ether, Holy Spirit, and Holy Ghost," *Improvement Era* 12 (Mar. 1909): 391–94.

expanding universe remains unchanged due to a continuous creation of matter and the observable universe is practically the same at any time and any place. Widtsoe argued that in the long run God himself is governed by physical laws. In the eternal sense, God is not the universe's creator, he is its organizer. Drawing on Herbert Spencer, as he did in *Joseph Smith as Scientist*, Widtsoe argued that the universe has developed toward increasing complexity. Widtsoe correlated this view with the LDS doctrine of eternal progression. As humans acquire more knowledge, they also acquire power. This increasing power facilitates, through the endless acquisition of knowledge, the endless—that is, eternal—development of mankind.[52]

Human beings, Widtsoe wrote, might not yet comprehend the creation process since they have not yet developed the complex understanding that God has. In general terms, Widtsoe explicated "great forces, existing in the universe, and set into ceaseless operation by the directing intelligence of God, assembled and brought into place the materials constituting the earth, until, in the course of long periods of time, this sphere was fitted for the abode of man." Widtsoe emphasized that in creating the universe and the earth, God had worked through natural law, "the forces of nature act[ing] steadily but slowly in the accomplishment of great works" under God's direction.[53]

Widtsoe also discussed the creation of human beings. He wrote that we should interpret as figurative the biblical account of God creating man from the earth's dust and infusing the breath of life into inert material. We did not, he said, know the exact method God used in creating humans, and at our current stage of development we could not know them. Moreover, such knowledge is not "vital to a clear understanding of the plan of salvation."[54]

Widtsoe then turned to the fall of Adam and Eve. Drawing from an interpretation of the Book of Mormon, Widtsoe argued that the Fall came through natural law and that the biblical account of the Fall, like that of the Creation, was only figurative. In the Fall, Adam and Eve committed "no essential sin" except as an effect follows the

---

52. John A. Widtsoe, *A Rational Theology as Taught by The Church of Jesus Christ of Latter-day Saints* (Salt Lake City: General Priesthood Committee, 1915), iii, 3, 10, 20–22.

53. Widtsoe, *Rational Theology*, 45–46.

54. Widtsoe, *Rational Theology*, 45–46.

violation of any physical law whether deliberate or not. Rather, the "so-called curse" on Adam was actually only an opportunity for eternal progression.[55]

Widtsoe moved to a discussion of Latter-day Saint doctrine that originated in Joseph Smith's 1844 King Follett discourse that he delivered as a memorial to a valued Saint and in the Book of Abraham in the Pearl of Great Price. In the King Follett sermon Smith said:

> God himself He was once a man like us; yea, that God himself, the Father of us all, dwelt on an earth, the same as Jesus Christ Himself did; and I will show it from the Bible. ... and is an exalted man, and sits enthroned in yonder heavens! ... and you have got to learn how to be gods yourselves, and to be kings and priests to God, the same as all gods have done before you, namely, by going from one small degree to another."

In contemplating the creation of the universe: "The head God called together the Gods and sat in grand council to bring forth the world." They organized the world from preexisting matter, they did not create it from nothing.[56]

Smith spoke further on the origin and destiny of human beings. He preached:

> All learned men and the doctors of divinity say that God created it [the immortal spirit of humans] in the beginning; but it is not so. ... God made a tabernacle and put a spirit into it, and it became a living soul. ... The mind or the intelligence which man possesses is co-equal [co-eternal] with God himself. ... The intelligence of spirits had no beginning, neither will it have an end.[57]

Relying on Smith's views, Widtsoe insisted that God created neither the universe nor human beings from nothing. Moreover, as Smith preached, man must be co-eternal with God. God did not operate in a mysterious way, Widtsoe wrote. Rather, he operated on

---

55. Widtsoe, *Rational Theology*, 46–48; see also 2 Ne. 2: 22–23.

56. *History of the Church of Jesus Christ of Latter-day Saints, Period I: History of Joseph Smith, the Prophet by Himself*, ed. B. H. Roberts, 2nd ed., vol. 6 (Salt Lake City: Deseret Book Co., 1969), 305–7; Terryl Givens with Brian M. Hauglid, *The Pearl of Greatest Price: Mormonism's Most Controversial Scripture* (New York: Oxford University Press, 2019), 42–60; Moses 7–8, in PGP; See also Stan Larson, "The King Follett Discourse: A Newly Amalgamated Text," *BYU Studies* 18 (Winter 1978): 193–208.

57. *History of the Church*, 6:310–311. B. H. Roberts, the volume's editor, added the parenthetical "co-eternal," arguing that that is what Joseph Smith meant.

a level far advanced from humankind. Widtsoe said, "The man who progresses through his increase in knowledge and power becomes a collaborator with God." Humankind's progression was God's progression, and God procreated just as humans did. It follows, "we must also have a mother who possesses the attributes of Godhood."[58]

In the manuscript Widtsoe submitted for publication, he extended the argument far beyond things that the First Presidency felt comfortable endorsing as church doctrine. He had included a discussion of humans before they became spirit beings, and he presented a speculative view that there had been a time when there was no God. On December 7, 1914, when President Joseph F. Smith, who was then in Missouri, learned of Widtsoe's speculation, he telegraphed his first counselor, Anthon H., Lund, telling him to halt publication of *Rational Theology*. Lund secured the manuscript from Edward H. Anderson, who was overseeing publication for the General Priesthood Committee. After he read the text on the evolution of God from intelligence to superior being to God, Lund responded with the comment, "I do not like to think of a time when there was no God." President Smith eliminated those passages from the book as being too speculative.[59]

During the period from the 1890s through the first two decades of the twentieth century, church leaders and scholars spent considerable time considering the church's theology. Among those involved in addition to Widtsoe were James E. Talmage, a PhD in geology and chemistry and president of the University of Utah; Frederick J. Pack, PhD and a University of Utah geology professor; B. H. Roberts, who held an undergraduate degree from the University of Deseret but was largely self-educated; and J. C. Homans, a non-Mormon writing at times under the pseudonym of Robert C. Webb, PhD. Homans did not have a PhD, and his writings created problems for the church.

In 1909, the year following the publication of Widtsoe's *Joseph Smith as Scientist*, the First Presidency issued a statement titled "The Origin of Man." Orson F. Whitney wrote the first draft of the

58. Widtsoe, *Rational Theology*, 26–27, 61–62, 64, 146.
59. Anthon H. Lund, Journal, Dec 7, 11, 1914, History Library, Church of Jesus Christ of Latter-day Saints, Salt Lake City.

statement, but Widtsoe, Talmage, and BYU President George H. Brimhall reviewed and edited the draft. Like Widtsoe, they considered the biblical account allegorical, and viewed Adam as the first man. The statement uses the terms "class" and "order," as Widtsoe had done, but it is not clear that they meant them scientifically, as Widtsoe did.[60]

Widtsoe enjoyed a pleasant personal life during these years. Leah organized and facilitated numerous dinners and receptions for guests of "national and international distinction." She bore six children while the family lived in Logan; unfortunately, only three lived to maturity.[61]

While building and maintaining his family, during the decade Widtsoe spent as president of USAC, he managed to finish a number of important tasks. He undid the mess generated by the battle over the consolidation of the University of Utah and USAC. He also helped USAC recover from the battle with the legislature Kerr had caused between 1905 and 1907 by trying to convert the agricultural college into a state university. The legislature simply would not support two universities, and the majority of legislators did not want to consolidate the two institutions. The consolidation never happened, and the transformation of USAC into a university was a task for the 1950s when the population of the state of Utah had become large enough to warrant it. The name change to Utah State University occurred in 1957.

During his tenure, Widtsoe facilitated the expansion of agricultural education and research, which he believed was the college's principal duty. By taking the results of research at the college and the extension service to practicing farmers, he helped to improve agriculture in the state as well as improve the image of the college. He turned around his own image with both the town and gown in the process. The publication of books on dry farming and irrigated farming provided information that helped farmers improve the practice of agriculture, the image of the college, and Widtsoe's own reputation as a leader in the field.

60. Joseph F. Smith, John R. Winder, and Anthon H. Lund, "The Origin of Man," *Improvement Era* 13 (Nov. 1909): 75–81.

61. Widtsoe, *Sunlit Land*, 124–25.

Widtsoe also worked to facilitate one of his goals: promoting his belief that religion and science were compatible and could reinforce one another. Unfortunately, although his proposal to link the concept of the luminiferous ether with the Holy Spirit may have seemed plausible at the time, in the long run it had to give way to quantum mechanics. More important was his work backed by his personal prestige in the introduction of a modified version of natural selection and progressive evolution into the discussion of LDS Church doctrine. Perhaps equally important, he contradicted the untenable position that the earth was only 6,000 years old, a doctrine that became increasingly indefensible as scientists made significant discoveries in fields such as anthropology, astronomy, biology, and other disciplines.

CHAPTER SEVEN

PRESIDENT OF THE
UNIVERSITY OF UTAH

After nine years as president of USAC, Widtsoe had no idea that his life would suddenly change. The change began on January 14, 1916, when Richard W. Young, chair of the executive committee of the Board of Regents of the University of Utah, called him to ask if he, as a personal favor, could meet with Widtsoe in Salt Lake City that evening. Widtsoe agreed, and when the two met, Young took him to a meeting of the regents' executive committee. The committee wasted little time in small talk but told him quite bluntly that President Joseph T. Kingsbury would retire as president of the University of Utah, and they had chosen him as president. As with President William J. Kerr at USAC, the regents were allowing Kingsbury to resign under pressure.[1]

Widtsoe was reluctant to accept the appointment. He had accomplished a great deal in Logan, and he and his family were happy living there. He knew it would be more expensive to live in Salt Lake City. He understood as well that his salary would be $2,000 per year less as president of the U of U. At Utah State he had improved the standards for admission, facilitated outreach to farmers, and published books on dry farming and irrigation farming. He was, after all, a biochemist who had devoted himself to the study of biological processes in plants and the relation of plants to the soil, water, nutrients, and air. He expected when he retired as president he could

---

1. John A. Widtsoe, *In a Sunlit Land: The Autobiography of John A. Widtsoe* (Salt Lake City: Milton R. Hunter and G. Homer Durham, 1952), 125.

occupy the laboratory and continue his research in the building on the campus named for him.[2]

In his meeting with the executive committee, he explained that he would remain active in the church. In his educational position, however, he would "keep my views on religion to myself." He advised the executive committee "that they would prefer another type of man, perhaps a so-called 'jack-Mormon,' one a Mormon in name but not in practice." They ignored him and pressed him to take the position. He agreed.[3]

Widtsoe understood that his appointment would thrust him into an academic controversy that made the problems he had encountered at USAC seem like a Sunday afternoon stroll. Even though Kingsbury had drifted away from the LDS Church, charges of church influence clouded the atmosphere at the U. The problems were exacerbated since a number of prominent Latter-day Saints were members of the board. Richard W. Young, a stake president, was chair of the University's board of regents and Anthon H. Lund, first counselor in the church's First Presidency, was a member of the board as well.

Charges of LDS interference were only part of the issues that generated controversy at the U. At the university commencement services in 1914, valedictorian Milton H. Sevy gave an address in which he criticized Utah's "ultra-conservatism" in general and Utah governor William Spry in particular. Following Sevy's address, Spry sent a letter to the board of regents expressing strong indignation over the speech, and Kingsbury publicly disapproved of the speech as well.[4]

From the summer of 1914 through January 1916, the relations among administration, faculty, and student body descended into persistent turmoil. Fueling the dissension, Kingsbury undertook to demote or fire a number of professors. In February 1915, Kingsbury "demoted" George M. Marshall, from English department chairman to department faculty member because, in his opinion, Marshall "had not retained the full efficiency and vigor that is expected and demanded of Professors and instructors." Kingsbury recommended

---

2. Widtsoe, *Sunlit Land,* 125–27.

3. Widtsoe, *Sunlit Land,* 143–44.

4. American Association of University Professors, "Preliminary Statement," 63, at aaup.org (accessed Aug. 11, 2021).

that as English department chair the regents appoint Widtsoe's brother, Osborne J. P. Widtsoe. Both Marshall and Osborne Widtsoe had MA's in English from Harvard. Osborne was, however, a local LDS ward bishop and principal of LDS High School. Kingsbury generated additional controversy by asking the regents to fire Ansel A. Knowlton in physics, George C. Wise in modern languages, and Phil C. Bing and Charles W. Snow in English, apparently because he believed they had made derogatory remarks about the university and himself and Snow had assisted Sevy in preparing his speech.[5]

Members of the U faculty and student body responded with anger at Kingsbury's actions. Seventeen faculty members resigned. Among those who left the university were Byron Cummings, dean of the school of arts and sciences, and Frank E. Holman, dean of the law school. Dean of mines and engineering Joseph F. Merrill remained, but he spoke with Anthon Lund about the controversy: "He [Merrill] thought he [Kingsbury] does [not] draw his faculty to him," but had a strained relationship with them.[6]

On February 24, 1915, after Kingsbury had asked Osborne to take the English department chair, Osborne called on the church's First Presidency to ask their advice. They urged him to accept the appointment. In contrast, Francis M. Lyman, president of the Quorum of the Twelve Apostles, and his son Richard R. Lyman, a University of Utah faculty member, thought Osborne ought to promote peace at the university by declining the appointment. If he did not, they believed that the public would charge the church with using its influence to put a Mormon bishop on the university faculty.[7] Osborne accepted the appointment, and the public responded just as

---

5. Joseph H. Jeppson, "The Secularization of the University of Utah to 1920" (PhD diss., University of California, Berkeley, 1973), 159–65; "Conditions at the University of Utah," *School and Society* 1 (Mar. 27, 1915): 456–59.

6. Jeppson, "Secularization of the University of Utah," 159–65; "Conditions at the University of Utah," 456–59; Anthon H. Lund, Journal, Mar. 17, 19, 1915, History Library, Church of Jesus Christ of Latter-day Saints, Salt Lake City. Entries are also found in Anthon H. Lund, *Danish Apostle: The Diaries of Anthon H. Lund, 1890–1921*, ed. John P. Hatch (Salt Lake City: Signature Books/Smith-Pettit Foundation, 2006); American Association of University Professors, "Preliminary Statement," 73, 77. See also Casey Paul Griffiths, *Truth Seeker: The Life of Joseph F. Merrill: Scientist, Educator, and Apostle* (Provo, UT: Brigham Young University Religious Studies Center, 2021), 123.

7. Lund, Journal, Mar. 20, 1915.

the Lymans thought. Protesters "howled that Church interference had caused the whole trouble."[8]

Widtsoe thought the problem at the U went even deeper than the immediate controversy. During John R. Park's presidency (1869–92), most of the faculty were Latter-day Saints, but most "became luke-warm to religion of any kind." Widtsoe believed that non-Mormon faculty members, especially those who came from other states, had an unfriendly attitude toward the Latter-day Saints. Some made "de-rogatory" remarks in class about the church and its traditions. Widtsoe concluded that this background led the regents to offer the presidency to him. Whether he was right or not, "the unfortunate university upheaval had caused the disgraceful Mormon-Gentile controversy to flare into full light." In the midst of this brouhaha, Widtsoe's appointment as president added to the Mormon-non-Mormon con-troversy. Charges that the church had explicitly engineered Widtsoe's appointment were patently false. His stellar education, academic, and administrative accomplishments fully qualified him. Moreover, he believed and practiced "that a man's politics and religion is his own affair and should be kept out of his official work. He has no right to use his influence to teach religion nor ir-religion in the classroom."[9]

At first, a majority of the regents supported Kingsbury's actions, and they refused to become involved in the controversy. In an at-tempt to persuade them that they were wrong, on March 17, 1915, professors Wise and Knowlton met with the regents. The regents asked them if they wanted to make a statement. They said they would, but only if the regents agreed to investigate conditions at the U. The regents refused, so the two did not present their views.[10]

The regents' refusal did not put the issue to rest. Nationally prominent journals published articles about the controversy, and the recently organized American Association of University Professors (AAUP) sent Johns Hopkins University professor Arthur O. Love-joy to investigate.[11] Lovejoy was appalled because, in addition to the

---

8. Widtsoe, *Sunlit Land*, 131.
9. Widtsoe, *Sunlit Land*, 142–43.
10. Lund, Journal, Feb. 26, Mar. 17, 1915.
11. Lund, Journal, Apr. 17, May 5, 1915; "Discussion and Correspondence: Meth-ods of the Board of Regents of the University of Utah," *School and Society* 3 (Feb. 26, 1916): 314–15.

firings, Kingsbury had also adopted a policy that interfered with free speech. He reportedly prohibited any negative political and religious speech. Lovejoy's report criticized Kingsbury for not understanding that adverse reactions to political and religious speech were not grounds for suppressing freedom of expression on any question.[12]

After submitting his preliminary report, Lovejoy recommended that AAUP appoint a committee to conduct a full investigation. In response, the AAUP sent a committee of seven professors under the chairmanship of Edwin R. A. Seligman of Columbia University. After interviewing numerous people about the issues, including Kingsbury, faculty members, and members of the regents, the committee issued its report. Committee members were astounded by the regents' policy that they could remove professors for no cause except that "when serious 'friction' arises between university officials and teachers, the governing body [the regents] should consider only the past and the inferential future value to the institution of the services of the persons concerned, and should not consider the question 'who is right and who is wrong in the disagreement.'"[13] Responding to this statement of regents' policy, the AAUP committee opined: "Such a rule of action on the part of a governing board contains the potency of grave injury to the institution under its control, not less than of grave injustice to individuals; for a publicly proclaimed indifference of the governing body to the question of justice as between individuals is sure to cause damaging resentments and a loss of public confidence."[14]

In addition to the AAUP report, U of U faculty members expressed their view of the dispute in various venues. Law school dean Frank Holman, for instance, gave a speech that he published in *School and Society* in which he charged Kingsbury with a systematic but covert policy of repression. He said that Kingsbury instituted a policy of prohibiting any political activity that might offend others. He wrote that Kingsbury told professors not to speak openly including at a Democratic rally or to express an opinion on monetary

---

12. "Discussion and Correspondence: Methods of the Board of Regents of the University of Utah," 314–15.

13. American Association of University Professors, "Preliminary Statement," 22.

14. AAUP, "Preliminary Statement," 22.

policy. Kingsbury, Holman said, took adverse action on reports of speech of which he disapproved without holding hearings to determine whether the charges were true or not.[15]

Kingsbury denied much of what Holman had written while defending his repression of political speech. He said that state law prohibited professors from engaging in partisan political or religious controversy. He denied Holman's other charges except the assertion that he asked one professor not to give a political speech. In his defense, he said that his recommendation was advisory rather than prohibitory.[16]

The University Alumni Association weighed in by appointing a committee of twenty-five to investigate the charges, firings, and resignations. The committee sided with the professors.[17]

Throughout 1915, like a disturbed hive of hornets, controversy buzzed around the university and the state, creating such a severe disturbance that Kingsbury decided to resign. In January 1916, Kingsbury wrote and informed the regents that he declined to "stand for reappointment as President of the university." On their meeting of January 20, 1916, the regents voted to accept Kingsbury's resignation and appointed him professor emeritus of chemistry. Understandably, the controversy and the outcome caused Kingsbury considerable anguish. After he resigned, the faculty offered Kingsbury a vote of confidence, but he left the university a defeated, emotionally damaged man.[18] On January 24, 1916, Kingsbury met with Anthon Lund, who tried to console him. Kingsbury told Lund that their discussion "had done him good."[19]

The regents' executive committee told Widtsoe they planned to appoint him as president on January 14, 1916, but none except the executive committee knew of Kingsbury's resignation and Widtsoe's appointment until January 18, and the entire board did not consider his appointment until January 20.[20]

15. Frank E. Holman, "The Policy of Repression, Suspicion, and Opportunism at the University of Utah," *School and Society* 1 (Apr. 10, 1915): 512–22.

16. Joseph T. Kingsbury, "Discussion and Correspondence: Dean Holman's Criticism of the Administration of the University of Utah," *School and Society* 1 (May 22, 1915): 745–47.

17. Lund, Journal, Apr. 7, 13, 1915.

18. Lund, Journal, Jan. 18, 20, 24, 1916.

19. Lund, Journal, Jan. 20, 24, 1916.

20. Lund, Journal, Jan. 20, 1916.

On January 20, after the regents had completed the discussion of Kingsbury's resignation, Waldemar Van Cott moved to appoint Widtsoe as president of the University of Utah. All of the members present except William W. Armstrong and Ernest Bamberger agreed. The two regents proposed, instead, to appoint a five-person search committee to select a new president. In a six-to-four vote, the regents agreed to appoint Widtsoe. In addition to Armstrong and Bamberger, George C. Whitmore and Nathan T. Porter voted against Widtsoe's appointment.[21]

Although Kingsbury resigned in January 1916, the regents had already begun to take steps to improve the relationship between them, the president, and the faculty. Nearly ten months earlier on March 27, 1915, Richard Young, the regents' chair, had appointed a committee on faculty relations. The faculty relations committee authorized the university faculty to organize an administrative council that would include faculty representatives. A faculty committee drafted a proposal for the administrative council that they submitted to the regents' faculty relations committee. They proposed that the administrative council consist of the university president and all the college and school deans. These were to serve as *ex officio* council members. In addition, seven faculty members elected by the faculty were to serve on the administrative council as voting members. The document said:

> The Administrative Council shall determine, subject to the approval of the Board of Regents, all matters pertaining to the educational policy and educational administration of the University.... All appointments, removals or changes in rank of members of the teaching force shall be made upon recommendation of the President to the Administrative Council after consultation with heads of Departments and Deans of Schools concerned.... All legislative power shall be vested in the Faculty of the University.

After the regents' faculty relations committee considered the plan, they informed Dean Milton Bennion of the School of Education that they had accepted the proposal. The regents, however, refused to apply the administrative council proposal to those cases that came before it in March 1915. This meant, of course, that the administrative

---

21. Lund, Journal, Jan. 20, 1916.

council could not investigate the controversy over Kingsbury's actions and the firing or resignation of faculty members.[22]

On March 13, 1916, after the regents had accepted Kingsbury's resignation and agreed to appoint Widtsoe as president, they met with him at the University of Utah. Widtsoe told them "that he hoped to have the full confidence of all the regents, for otherwise he did not feel he would succeed." He gave the regents the draft of a proposed constitution he wanted to adopt for the university. He told the regents that the constitution "would make plain the duties of all connected with the institution." He said he had modeled the constitution after the University of Illinois constitution that had been in effect for three years. Lund wrote that he "felt proud of Bro. Widtsoe when I saw him take hold of this task." On the way home with Lund, Armstrong (who had previously opposed Widtsoe's appointment) told Lund, "He will suit me for there is push in him and ability to carry through his ideas."[23]

As he did when he assumed the presidency of USAC, Widtsoe asked for and received a blessing from the First Presidency of the church. Joseph F. Smith gave Widtsoe the blessing. Leah accompanied him to the meeting with the First Presidency, and she asked for a blessing as well, which Anthon Lund gave her. Widtsoe was not well at the time, so Smith "advised him to go to Honolulu and take a rest." In May, John and Leah sailed to Honolulu for "a three-months rest."[24]

Because of the controversy over Kingsbury's administrative style, the appointment of Osborne, the firing of four professors, and the resignation of seventeen other professors, Widtsoe's appointment threw him into a "mess." "The fight had unnerved" the faculty. In addition, they had "to deal with a new president, strange to them." One professor whom Widtsoe did not name "was bitterly disappointed" when the regents did not appoint him president, and he declined to support Widtsoe. One of the deans approached Widtsoe, asking him "to sign a document which gave him full control over more than one-half of the faculty." Widtsoe's "refusal left him soured."[25]

22. AAUP, "Preliminary Statement," 49–51.
23. Lund, Journal, Mar. 13, 1916.
24. Lund, Journal, Apr. 19, 1916; Widtsoe, *Sunlit Land*, 127.
25. Widtsoe, *Sunlit Land*, 132–33.

Although Kingsbury's actions had not pleased the alumni, most were not inclined to support Widtsoe either. He was, some said, a president who had served as president of a "cow college" in Logan. Widtsoe concluded that he had "to go to work with a smile and trust the corrective power of time and honest effort." Over time, Widtsoe ingratiated himself with the alumni and faculty as he had with the regents, and the university community gave him "full support" and "every courtesy that I could expect."[26]

Widtsoe recognized that the state legislature had passed a series of acts that affected the university, but that neither the regents nor the administration had drafted rules that put the laws into practice. As a result, "almost my first task, even before entering officially upon my University duties, was to formulate a series of Board rules and regulations for the guidance of all connected with the institution." In this, he must have been referring to the "constitution" mentioned in Anthon Lund's journal. In his autobiography, Widtsoe wrote that the rules he formulated "were printed and have been in force ever since, with such amendments as the years have brought." These brought "certainty and order [and] made me feel easier about my work, and, in fact, were a protection to the university faculty."[27]

Widtsoe knew, however, that he still had to cope with the anti-Mormon attitude of some faculty and regents. He wrote that he "accidentally overheard two non-Mormon regents, among the most eminent men of the State, conversing on this subject." One said, "'We must take over the University and train the young people away from Mormonism.' 'Yes,' answered the other, 'you are right. That's our next job, to secure full control of the institution, secure a non-Mormon president and teachers, and educate the students away from Mormon beliefs. The State will then be ours."[28] Clearly, he had to convince people with such views, whether regents, alumni, faculty, students, or the public at large, that he could leave his religious persuasion at home or in a church setting while serving as university president.

Widtsoe firmly believed that anti- and pro-Mormon rhetoric had no place in the university. He believed that until faculty and

---

26. Widtsoe, *Sunlit Land*, 133–34.
27. Widtsoe, *Sunlit Land*, 134–35.
28. Widtsoe, *Sunlit Land*, 144.

others left "their religious prejudices at home, ... it cannot rise to its destiny to be the great intermountain university."[29]

In spite of the anti-Mormon attitudes of some in the community, because of Widtsoe's commitment to academic freedom, he did not care whether faculty members belonged to the LDS Church, another church or religion, or no church at all. He thought that neither religious or irreligious preaching had any place in a public university. As a corollary, he deplored those who sought in their classes to undermine or belittle the faith of any student. These convictions did not affect his personal beliefs and practices. As a personal matter, he believed that faith in God, no matter which faith, made anyone a better person. He also believed that professors with faith were happier and that they did a better job of "the building of character, and fitting of youth for the best matter of living."[30]

Before he assumed the U's presidency, he knew that a number of anti-Mormons insisted that the church leadership influenced to a great degree the hiring of faculty and the operation of the university. He believed that was generally untrue. During his tenure as president of the U of U, he received only two requests to hire any faculty members. Because of one request, he hired a British immigrant, David Hughes, "an accomplished wood-carver," to work at the university. In the other case, he could not hire Captain George H. Curry, also a British immigrant, when he was asked to do so, to teach French because there was no vacancy in the department.[31]

While working to develop additional friends and supporters among the regents and establishing faculty government, Widtsoe undertook a number of initiatives. Concerned about the university's outreach beyond Salt Lake City, he secured board approval for the establishment of an extension division. The division offered correspondence classes; faculty members also taught classes in person throughout the state.[32]

In addition to the extension division, Widtsoe turned his efforts to improving the university's medical school. He added programs on

---

29. Widtsoe, *Sunlit Land*, 147.
30. Widtsoe, *Sunlit Land*, 146.
31. Widtsoe, *Sunlit Land*, 146–47.
32. Widtsoe, *Sunlit Land*, 135.

child health and welfare as part of the extension division. He had a more difficult problem with the medical school to solve, however. The university's medical school offered only two years of instruction instead of the usual four. The American Medical Association had granted the school an A rating but threatened to revoke that rating because of the unusually few years of instruction. He succeeded in convincing the AMA to allow the U to retain the A rating by making several trips to Chicago to meet with AMA executives. The university also constructed a new medical building that continued in use during Widtsoe's lifetime.[33]

Widtsoe believed strongly in the need for adequate "training in the fundamental sciences for persons who are allowed to practice officially as healers of disease." It is somewhat difficult to understand his thoughts on the matter, but it seems that he believed that doctors and medical schools often passed traditions on to one another without sufficient blind tests and laboratory examination to verify their effectiveness. He thought also that medical practitioners did not devote themselves sufficiently to "the preventive field," that is, trying to keep people healthy so they would not need remedial medicine so frequently.[34] He would later consider this problem in the reinterpretation of the church's Word of Wisdom's health code on which he and Leah published.

Widtsoe promoted the growth of the university and the increased educational capability of the faculty. In order to increase the expansion of business opportunities in the "trade and industry" of Utah's natural resources, he convinced the regents to authorize the establishment of a school of commerce. He also encouraged the expansion of post-graduate study by urging the faculty to offer post-graduate degrees and to seek post-graduate degrees themselves at other institutions.[35]

In addition, Widtsoe introduced a system of general education that required students to take classes in fields other than their major. He instituted this requirement as a modification of the elective system that Charles W. Eliot had introduced at Harvard.[36]

---

33. Widtsoe, *Sunlit Land*, 135–36.

34. Widtsoe, *Sunlit Land*, 147–48.

35. Widtsoe, *Sunlit Land*, 137–38.

36. Widtsoe, *Sunlit Land*, 138–39.

Widtsoe took an interest in the extracurricular activities of the students by attending athletic events, dances, and other student functions. To reduce the emphasis on leadership by returned LDS missionaries, he convinced them to organize an honor fraternity called Delta Phi to which all former Christian missionaries, not just Latter-day Saints, could belong.[37]

Widtsoe had a more difficult time in securing appropriations for the university's expansion than he had had at USAC. Nevertheless, in addition to the medical building, the legislature approved the construction of observatory buildings, a training school, a dining hall, and other buildings.[38]

Even before Widtsoe assumed the university presidency, during the summer of 1914 World War I had broken out in Europe. In April 1917, after Germany declared unrestricted submarine warfare and carried out some raids, the United States declared war on Germany and Austria-Hungary. Under federal direction, men studying at the U were enrolled in an organization called the Student Army Training Corps. When the Spanish Flu broke out in the United States in 1918, Widtsoe ordered the students to return to their homes. Countermanding his instructions, despite the epidemic, the army ordered the students back to campus. As a result, the flu spread rapidly through their ranks and eighteen SATC men died.[39]

During the war, Governor Simon Bamberger appointed Widtsoe to the Utah State Council of Defense. The council organized committees to address wartime needs for functions such as finance, war loans, publicity, sanitation, food supply and conservation, industry, labor, military affairs, and transportation. In addition, Widtsoe chaired the Salt Lake City food production committee. In that capacity, he urged citizens to plant crops on the city's vacant lots, for which he helped devised means of providing irrigation. People in Salt Lake City grew about $600,000 worth of food on the lots (about $11.3 million in today's dollars).[40]

During the war, in order to make conditions more convenient for

37. Widtsoe, *Sunlit Land*, 138–39.
38. Widtsoe, *Sunlit Land*, 139.
39. Widtsoe, *Sunlit Land*, 139–40.
40. Widtsoe, *Sunlit Land*, 139–40; On the State Council of Defense, see archives. utah.gov (accessed Aug. 16, 2021).

students leaving for and returning from the war, the National Educational Association recommended that universities change their schedule from semesters to quarters. Widtsoe instituted that change at the U.[41]

As an aspect of his tenure as president, Widtsoe also discussed his views on education. He believed that the progress of students from elementary school, high school, and college or university should be fluid. Many colleges have entrance requirements, and at the time high school had them as well. He believed that in addition to such subjects as history and English, students should gain a basic knowledge of the sciences and should understand the functioning of the various bodily organs.[42]

Widtsoe had reasonable ideas about the function of teachers in a university. He felt that they should recognize that most students would not go on after graduation to obtain master's or doctoral degrees. He believed that teachers should organize their class material so that average students could comprehend their subjects. The teachers, in his view, should clearly differentiate between facts and theory in ways that the students could understand the difference. Too many teachers, he thought, prided themselves on how many students they could fail. Such a practice, he believed, undermined the purpose of education.[43]

While serving as president, Widtsoe also worked as a volunteer in the educational community. He served as senior member of the Utah State Board of Education. He deplored when later presidents of colleges and universities were removed from the state board. He served for two terms beginning in 1918 as president of the Utah Education Association. He praised teachers for their willingness to serve at the time when their salaries were lower than those for "tradesmen and garbage collectors." He also served on the pan-American states organization and presented papers at their meetings.[44]

During the same time and in succeeding years, he published two books for the church, and he continued his church service. He

---

41. Widtsoe, *Sunlit Land*, 140–41.
42. Widtsoe, *Sunlit Land*, 148–50.
43. Widtsoe, *Sunlit Land*, 151–52.
44. Widtsoe, *Sunlit Land*, 152–53.

collected the sermons of President Joseph F. Smith into a volume titled *Gospel Doctrine*, and compiled some of Brigham Young's talks in *Brigham Young's Discourses*. He had a close relationship with Joseph F. Smith, whom he admired as a person and leader. That Brigham Young had "learned the restored gospel" from Joseph Smith impressed Widtsoe.[45] He continued to serve on the church's General Board of the YMMIA, and as chair of the MIA committee drafting plans for young men of high school and college age. The committee organized the M Men (Mutual Men) program of the MIA which provided certain objectives for young men to meet to help steady "the religious pulse of youth." He also chaired a group to suggest ways to improve the church's temple and genealogical work. The committee devised the "Index Bureau" name-cataloguing system that helped in genealogical research.[46]

Widtsoe's wife, Leah, committed herself to community work as well. She served as president of the Salt Lake City Federation of Women's Clubs while also hosting numerous dinners and luncheons in their home.[47]

Regarding home, Widtsoe found serving as U of U president difficult. Unlike the USAC, the U of U had no president's home at the time. The Widtsoes lived in rented homes until, after three years as president, they were able to construct their own house near the university. Since Widtsoe had a much lower salary than he had received at Utah State, he had to rely on a combination of salary, savings, and frugality.[48]

While he served as university president, on Thursday, March 17, 1921, Widtsoe's life changed again in an unanticipated way. Elder Richard R. Lyman, a member of the Quorum of the Twelve Apostles, asked him to come to his office in the church's downtown office building. Lyman took him to the temple to the meeting of the First Presidency and the Twelve Apostles. In the meeting President

---

45. Widtsoe, *Sunlit Land*, 153–54; Joseph F. Smith, *Gospel Doctrine: Selections from The Sermons and Writings of Joseph F. Smith* (Salt Lake City: Deseret Book Co., 1963, orig. 1919); Brigham Young, *Discourses of Brigham Young*, ed. John A. Widtsoe (Salt Lake City: Deseret Book, 1925).

46. Widtsoe, *Sunlit Land*, 155.

47. Widtsoe, *Sunlit Land*, 154.

48. Widtsoe, *Sunlit Land*, 154–55.

Heber J. Grant called Widtsoe to fill the vacancy in the Twelve occasioned by the death of Anthon Lund and by the call of Anthony W. Ivins of the Twelve to the First Presidency (where he replaced Lund). Although he thought intensely about such a call, Widtsoe accepted it as he had every other call for service in the church. After he had accepted, Grant ordained him an apostle and set him apart as a member of the Quorum of the Twelve Apostles. Church members ratified Widtsoe's new appointment at general conference on April 3, 1921. George Thomas, an active Latter-day Saint, succeeded him as U of U president on June 30, 1921, under the same type of anti-Mormon cloud that Widtsoe had had to contend with.[49]

Widtsoe's service at the university had occurred during exceptionally trying times. Upon entering the presidency, he struggled with the strife caused by the controversy over Kingsbury's administration. In dealing with this and other problems, Widtsoe changed the university's administration. Presenting a document titled *Regulations of the Faculty of the University of Utah*, he turned virtually every aspect of university administration to the faculty under his chairmanship.[50] In contrast with Kingsbury's dictatorial rule—in which the president relied only on regents' approval for changes— Widtsoe instituted a democratic system of administration in which the president worked with the faculty under regents' guidance. World War I disrupted the university's functioning during 1917 and 1918, and the subsequent Spanish Flu epidemic caused sickness and death among the student body. In spite of these setbacks, Widtsoe presided over the construction of new buildings and retained the medical school's accreditation. Reaching out to the public, he established an extension division and encouraged teachers to organize classes away from the campus.

49. Widtsoe, *Sunlit Land*, 156–57.
50. Alan K. Parish, *John A. Widtsoe: A Biography* (Salt Lake City: Deseret Book Co., 2003), 235.

CHAPTER EIGHT

A NEW APOSTLE

From 1921 until his death in 1952, Widtsoe served as one of the fifteen highest ranking leaders in the LDS Church. Since the death of church founder Joseph Smith in June 1844, and the meeting of Saints in Nauvoo on August 8 to identify Smith's successor—upon the passing of a church president, the Quorum of the Twelve Apostles has assumed the leadership of the church and had called the next president. Moreover, since December 1847, the quorum had invariably called its senior member and quorum president as church president.

Although Widtsoe accepted the apostolic call because of his testimony of the gospel, he realized that his financial condition had taken an even deeper hit than when he transferred from USAC to the U of U. In his autobiography he wrote that "the Church allowance, supposed to be sufficient for a modest support, was about a third of what my annual earnings had been, going on to two decades."[1] Research by D. Michael Quinn shows that in 1921, LDS Church apostles received an income of $4,020 per year, an amount almost precisely one third of $12,000.[2] Even with the much higher salary, at the University of Utah Widtsoe's "university expenses had exceeded the income." When Widtsoe was called to the apostleship, he had recently "built a home near the university." Such expenses had bitten deeply into previous savings, and two of his "older children [Anna Gaarden, b. 1899, and Karl Marselius, called Marsel, b.

---

1. John A. Widtsoe, *In a Sunlit Land: The Autobiography of John A. Widtsoe* (Salt Lake City: Milton R. Hunter and G. Homer Durham, 1952), 161.

2. D. Michael Quinn, *The Mormon Hierarchy: Wealth and Corporate Power* (Salt Lake City: Signature Books, 2017), 13.

1902] were ready for missions." To reduce expenses, he sold his car and "dismissed" his servants.[3]

Widtsoe did have some additional income because he served as a director of a number of firms and institutions. Some of these were Beneficial Life Insurance, Big Four Consolidated Mining and Milling Company, Crescent Eagle Oil Company, Eddington-Cope Radio Corporation, Inland Fertilizer Company, Mountain State Development Company, Phillips Petroleum Company, Silver Lake Company, State Savings and Loan Association, Utah Bentonite Corporation, and William Budge Memorial Hospital. He also had some US government securities. Actually, Widtsoe served as an officer in a larger number of businesses while he lived in Logan than while he was an apostle. He also served in a number of charitable, public service, and professional organizations. These included, in addition to the hospital, the Salt Lake Chamber of Commerce, Friar's Club, Utah State Historical Society, Western States Reclamation Commission, Santa Fe Conference that wrote the Colorado River Compact, Utah State Water Storage Commission, Utah Public Health Association, Committee of Special Advisors to the Bureau of Reclamation, Utah Tuberculosis Association, Utah State Water and Power Board, Royal Commission on the South Saskatchewan Project.[4] He also published books that might have earned him royalties, except that he gave the money to the church.[5]

As an apostle, Widtsoe also lost one advantage he previously had in his positions as a collegiate president. In those positions he "had had much freedom of initiative," and he had "ample secretarial help." While serving as an apostle, for many years he had to share a secretary with others.[6]

Widtsoe learned quite rapidly the burden he had assumed by accepting the call as an apostle. He found that "there is no Sabbath, or day of rest." In the second weekend after his ordination, he "was asked to conduct a stake quarterly conference." In 1921 the church

---

3. Widtsoe, *Sunlit Land*, 161–62.

4. Widtsoe, *Sunlit Land*, 161–62; D. Michael Quinn, *The Mormon Hierarchy: Extensions of Power* (Salt Lake City: Signature Books, 1997), 715–16; Quinn, *The Mormon Hierarchy: Wealth and Corporate Power*, 447–75.

5. Widtsoe, *Sunlit Land*, 163.

6. Widtsoe, *Sunlit Land*, 163.

had 83 stakes. The number increased over time so that by 1952, when he died, the church had 202 stakes. At the time, each stake held conferences four times a year. The First Presidency expected someone from the Quorum of the Twelve Apostles or First Council of the Seventy to conduct each of them personally, if at all possible. An apostle or seventy might take with him a member of one of the general boards or, after its organization, someone from the Church Welfare Committee. After the formation of the Assistants to the Twelve, one of them might accompany the apostle, or, if no apostle was available, one of them might conduct the conference. With the increasing number of stakes, the fifteen members of the First Presidency and Twelve had to attend and conduct stake quarterly conferences virtually every weekend of the year.[7]

Widtsoe learned of the enervating task of conducting stake conferences. He had to conduct "council meetings, [make] visits with the people, [do] preaching and ordinations." He wrote that it took about two days after the conference "to return to normal." Unfortunately, he had no time to recuperate because he had to attend to "office duties [that] have accumulated." He was convinced that sometime in the future "stakes [would have] no visitors from headquarters, [but that they would] have no diminution of spiritual enjoyment and help."[8] That is, of course, what has happened. In many cases, as of this writing, stake presidents conduct the conferences. In 1979, well after Widtsoe's death, the church leadership reduced the number of stake conferences to two each year.

When Widtsoe met the stake president at the first conference he conducted, he was delayed because his train arrived late. The stake president told him that they had already held one conference at which no general authority visitor attended. Widtsoe asked him "how they had fared at the one conference when they were alone." The stake president responded, emotionally, that they had "such an outpouring of the Holy Spirit" as at no other conference.[9]

Widtsoe thought that in spite of the burden carried by general

---

7. Widtsoe, *Sunlit Land*, 164; Deseret News, *2011 Church Almanac* (Salt Lake City: Deseret News, n.d.), 191–92.

8. Widtsoe, *Sunlit Land*, 165.

9. Widtsoe, *Sunlit Land*, 166.

authorities in conducting quarterly stake conferences, it was important that they should do so. The authorities had the opportunity to
teach the gospel to the rising generation and refresh the older ones.
"In the stake quarterly conferences," Widtsoe believed, "the visiting
member of the General Authorities can reach more people with his
message than at any other time, except at general conferences." I
suspect that the visits to stake conferences were more important because the meetings were smaller than at general conference.

General conference sessions convened in the Salt Lake Tabernacle. The building held 3,500 persons. At the time of Widtsoe's call in
1921, the church had 548,803 members. Although at the time most
members lived in the Intermountain West, only a few could attend
conference. By the time of Widtsoe's death in 1952, the church had
almost 1.2 million members. The number of members outside the
Intermountain West had begun to grow, but most still lived within
about three hundred miles of Salt Lake City, and most had access
either to personal cars or public transportation.[10]

Church leaders recognized that they needed to find some other
way to reach the membership in general conference. To do so, they
turned to technology. The church began broadcasting general conferences by radio in 1924 and by television in 1949. Although radio and
television can reach many more people than the number who could
fit in the tabernacle, a personally given sermon might be more effective than one transmitted over such media. These conditions made
authority visits to stake conference even more important.[11]

In addition to stake conference visits, the church's general authorities traveled to missions around the world. During Widtsoe's
apostleship, a general authority visited each mission about once each
year. In 1921 the church had twenty-five missions. The number grew
to forty-three in 1952.[12]

Widtsoe also met regularly with members of the First Presidency
and Twelve. On Wednesdays the Twelve, the First Council of the

10. *2011 Deseret News Church Almanac*, 191–92; Ryan Morgenegg, "A Historic
Look at the Church's Use of Media," *Church News*, churchofjesuschrist.org (accessed
Aug. 30, 2021).

11. *2011 Deseret News Church Almanac*, 191–92; Widtsoe, *Sunlit Land*, 166; Morgenegg, "Historic Look."

12. *2011 Deseret News Church Almanac*, 191–92; Widtsoe, *Sunlit Land*, 168.

Seventy, the Presiding Bishopric, and the Patriarch to the Church met together. Following the call of the Assistants to the Twelve in 1941, these brethren met with the others on Wednesday also. Every three months members of the Quorum of the Twelve Apostles held a quarterly meeting "for close exchange of thoughts and testimonies." The First Presidency and Quorum of the Twelve Apostles meet each Thursday in the Salt Lake Temple to pray together and discuss the needs and progress of the church. At each general conference, the Twelve and First Council of the Seventy meet with the mission presidents. Stake presidents and bishops in Salt Lake City and the surrounding area frequently asked general authorities to speak in their local congregations.[13]

These scheduled meetings and the visits to missions and to conduct stake conferences put a great deal of pressure on the church leadership. In spite of the demands on his time, Widtsoe believed that "such a heavy program would not be enjoyable were it not permeated by the spirit of the gospel." It furthered the "Lord's latter-day work," and "the spirit of peace, good will, and brotherly love" was "always present in the councils." In the meetings with other general authorities, although those present often voiced "sharp ... personal opinions," Widtsoe believed that "the sweetness of the gospel" overshadowed the differences. Widtsoe said that he had "never elsewhere ... felt so strongly the spirit of brotherhood." He wrote that he "repeatedly" felt the "evidences of the divine power that guides this work." He was particularly complimentary of President Heber J. Grant. He said that in several cases he felt "the mantle of the prophet" fall "on him." He felt the same way about later presidents George Albert Smith and David O. McKay with whom he also served. He felt certain that "the Lord" had chosen these men "to perform the necessary work on earth for the fulfillment of this plan." He recognized that "all men have their human weaknesses, but [believed] if they live righteously and obey God's laws they can be used for human uplift and progress."[14]

In addition to these scheduled assignments, other responsibilities fell on Widtsoe. In January 1922, less than a year after his call to the

13. Widtsoe, *Sunlit Land*, 168.
14. Widtsoe, *Sunlit Land*, 169–70.

Twelve, the First Presidency called him as church commissioner of education. He served until 1924. Adam S. Bennion who had been serving as superintendent of education since 1919 continued to serve under Widtsoe's direction and would replace Widtsoe in the Twelve after Widtsoe's death.[15]

At the time of his appointment, Widtsoe recognized that the church would soon stop supporting most of the academies that leaders and local officials had established since the late nineteenth century. He knew that the church would continue to shift its resources to support to seminaries built near high schools in Utah. The Granite Stake presidency, on the initiative of counselor Joseph F. Merrill, had founded the first seminary near Granite High School in 1912. At the time of Widtsoe's appointment as commissioner, the church had replicated the seminary model near twenty high schools, mostly in Utah. In these buildings, Church Education Department employees taught classes to high school students on gospel topics. Widtsoe knew that "many parents" opposed the closing of church sponsored academies because they wanted their children to go to religious schools. Nevertheless, he understood that financial demands made the continued operation of academies virtually impossible. The church did not have enough income, and members carried the burden of supporting two educational systems. They paid tithing and tuition to support the academies, and they supported public high schools through taxation. To address this duplication, "the seminary system ... seemed the nearest and best substitute."[16]

As the expansion of the seminary system continued, Latter-day Saints in many towns applied to have the church establish a seminary near their high school. Widtsoe hoped that this could be done "wherever our people are located." If the church did so, "all the children of all our people may have a chance to gain some special religious training" instead of the few who happen to live near the "special Church institutions."[17]

---

15. During this period, under the direction of the First Presidency and the Twelve Apostles, the church commissioner of education served as the highest official in the church educational system. The church superintendent of education served under the direction of the commissioner.

16. Widtsoe, *Sunlit Land*, 171.

17. Widtsoe, *Sunlit Land*, 171.

By late 1927 the church operated seventy seminaries. In Utah, most of the students attended seminary on what was called released time. Participating high schools allowed students to leave the high school for an hour to study and attend classes at a nearby seminary building. In 1929, the church instituted an early morning seminary system in Idaho for students who did not live in districts that permitted release time.[18]

In addition to discontinuing the support of academies, during the 1920s church leaders decided to withdraw from most higher education. So that Latter-day Saint students could continue to receive religious education, however, leadership arranged to construct buildings called institutes of religion near colleges and universities. They established the first institute near the University of Idaho in Moscow in 1926 with J. Wylie Sessions as instructor. At first, students received institute instruction in temporary quarters near the university. In 1929, however, the church constructed permanent institute buildings near the University of Idaho, and it built a similar structure near USAC in Logan.[19]

By the early 1930s, the church had largely abolished the academy system, and it retained only a fragment of its collegiate institutions. After several changes in name and function, fragments of the LDS University in Salt Lake City survived as the McCune School of Music and the LDS Business College. In 1926 the church closed Brigham Young College in Logan.[20]

After the outbreak of the Great Depression in the fall of 1929, the church moved more rapidly to dispose of its academies and to transfer its junior colleges to the states in which they were located.

18. Thomas G. Alexander, *Mormonism in Transition: A History of the Latter-day Saints, 1890–1930* (3rd ed. revised; Salt Lake City: Greg Kofford Books, 2015), 177; Scott C. Esplin, "Ideological or Financial? Academies or Seminaries and the Making of the Modern Church Educational System," in Matthew C. Godfrey and Michael Hubbard MacKay, eds., *Business and Religion: The Intersection of Faith and Finance* (Salt Lake City and Provo, UT: Brigham Young University/Deseret Book Co., 2019), 325.

19. Leon Hartshorn, "Mormon Education in the Bold Years" (EdD diss., Stanford University, 1965), 36; Leonard J. Arrington, "The Founding of the L.D.S. Institutes of Religion," *Dialogue: A Journal of Mormon Thought* 2 (Summer 1967): 213–43; Heber J. Grant, Diary, Feb. 27–28 and June 12, 1928, History Library, Church of Jesus Christ of Latter-day Saints, Salt Lake City.

20. Alexander, *Mormonism in Transition*, 178; "Latter-day Saints and Education: An Overview," Newsroom, newsroom.churchofjesuschrist.org (accessed Sep. 15, 2021).

In 1930, Joseph F. Merrill, then serving as church commissioner of education, announced that all church schools except Brigham Young University and Juarez Academy in Mexico would close in 1931. After some lobbying, Merrill succeeded in 1931 in inducing the Utah legislature to accept and operate Snow, Weber, and Dixie Junior Colleges. The state of Idaho refused to accept Ricks Junior College in Rexburg, and the church retained it.[21]

Eventually, the church sponsored college and university education at BYU in Provo, Ricks College in Rexburg, Idaho (now BYU-Idaho), and beginning in 1955, the Church College of Hawaii in Laie (now BYU-Hawaii), and LDS Business College (now Ensign College). In spite of eliminating the academies and most colleges in the United States, as of 2021 the church also maintained elementary and secondary schools in Mexico, Tonga, Samoa, Fiji and Kiribati.[22]

In 1934 church leaders again called Widtsoe as church commissioner of education. He served until 1936. Concerned about the quality of education in church institutions of higher learning, Widtsoe had urged the church to increase its appropriations for BYU. Under Widtsoe's commissionership, the church increased its annual appropriation to BYU from $200,000 to $300,000 per year. The remainder of its operating funds came from donations and from low faculty salaries. Franklin S. Harris, one of Widtsoe's protégés, was then serving as president, and worked energetically to improve the quality of the faculty and facilities. In the 1920s, only a minority of the BYU faculty held the PhD, but Harris managed to secure accreditation and to hire faculty of the stature of Lowry Nelson and Carl F. Eyring. He also urged faculty members to obtain graduate degrees; promoted faculty research, a requirement at any university; and convinced the church to construct a new library, which it named for President Grant.[23]

In addition to working to improve the church's educational system, Widtsoe continued his involvement in higher education. In the summers of 1924 through 1927, Widtsoe gave "a course of lectures on Western Rural Problems" at USAC. He focused particularly on

---

21. Alexander, *Mormonism in Transition*, 178–79.
22. See "Latter-day Saints and Education."
23. Alexander, *Mormonism in Transition*, 179.

irrigation, a topic on which he was arguably the world's authority. After 1936, Widtsoe again returned to USAC during summers for "about six years" to lecture on social and moral problems and "the Philosophy of Happiness."[24]

Widtsoe taught classes for the Church Education System as well, and at other venues at various times during the late 1920s and early 1930s. In the summer of 1928, he taught a course for seminary teachers at BYU's Aspen Grove summer school located near the North Fork of the Provo River a short distance east of Mt. Timpanogos. In 1934, he gave lectures to seminary teachers in Salt Lake City "on the philosophy and truth of Mormonism."[25]

In 1935, a year after Widtsoe's reappointment as church commissioner of education, church leaders received a proposal from the University of Southern California to offer a course on Mormonism at the university. USC decided to offer regular courses on Roman Catholicism, Judaism, Protestantism, and Mormonism. LDS officials asked Widtsoe to fill the position. The University of Southern California leadership wanted to place the study of "living religions in a systematic, dignified manner ... on an equal footing with all academic subjects." Widtsoe agreed to teach the classes, and he and Leah spent the academic year in Los Angeles. Widtsoe's classes "were well attended," and he considered the instruction "successful."[26]

In addition to teaching classes at USC, Widtsoe reached out to students in the various colleges and universities in the Los Angeles area. The administration of the University of California at Los Angeles included the church as "a member of the University Religious Conference." Widtsoe taught additional classes at Los Angeles City College. After Widtsoe left Southern California, G. Homer Durham (who married Widtsoe's daughter, Eudora, in 1936) and Byron Done took over instruction in Mormonism at USC, and they successfully continued and expanded the program.[27]

As part of his experience at the USC, Widtsoe prepared a textbook for courses on Mormonism. J. Wyley Sessions and Merrill D.

---

24. Widtsoe, *Sunlit Land*, 175.
25. Widtsoe, *Sunlit Land*, 175.
26. Widtsoe, *Sunlit Land*, 173.
27. Widtsoe, *Sunlit Land*, 174.

Clayson, collaborated with him by writing study questions and lists of supplementary readings to accompany Widtsoe's chapters.

Widtsoe titled the book *The Program of the Church of Jesus Christ of Latter-day Saints*, and he expected that in addition to students at USC, LDS seminaries, institutes, and mutual classes could use it as a text. The book progresses from the simple to the complex. The earliest chapters carry titles such as "What is Religion?," "Aim of Mormonism," "Happiness," the "Practices of the Church," "Motivating Elements," "Caring for the Body," and "Developing the Mind." Chapters include emphasis on activities and functions such as the emotions, spirituality, the family, social welfare, economics, the relation between the church and national government, activity and rotation in positions in the church, ordinances, daily life, and the church's organization and functions.

In some ways, sections of the book recapitulate Widtsoe's *Rational Theology* and anticipated his work in *Evidences and Reconciliations.* He argued that the human mind seeks explanations based on collecting information through the senses and applying reason. His scientific training is evident in statements like: "There is no place in the program of the Church of Jesus Christ of Latter-day Saints for conclusions not based on tested facts and straight thinking, nor for metaphysical speculations careless of time and space and facts. In religion, thinkers must have their feet on the ground" (185).

Thus, Widtsoe insisted that church members should examine the spiritual world in the same way they examine the physical world. He based his argument on Doctrine and Covenants Section 131:7: "There is no such a thing as immaterial matter. All spirit is matter, but it is more fine or pure, and can only be discerned by purer eyes" (188). He moved from that contention to a discussion of the universe, beginning with matter and energy. The information presented in the text indicates that Widtsoe may have been familiar with the work of Einstein and other scientists. He argued "that matter in its last state may be converted into energy, and is but a form of energy." He pointed out that some scientists believe that matter and energy "are interchangeable" (191).

Widtsoe's discussion of the universe seems deliberately to lead to chapter 28: "The Mystery of Origin." Significantly, both Widtsoe's text and the questions he references, posed by Sessions and Clayson (199–200), focus on science and logic rather than the Bible for answers to the question of the origin of life. Nevertheless, Widtsoe argued that "science, philosophy or religion [cannot yet] give complete answers to questions concerning the beginnings of life and the origin of man." Rather, he asserted: "The origin of man is known only in part.... These transcendental matters remain shrouded in mystery until more knowledge is obtained. There are doubtless many truths which are beyond the power of the finite human mind to comprehend." Widtsoe considers that "the distinguishing characteristics of a person is the possession of will, the power to accept or reject, to move or to stand still, to obey or to disobey" (191).

Since he believed that the answers science gave on the origin of humans on Earth are incomplete, he turned to the gospel for answers. Widtsoe discussed Adam and Eve and the "Plan of Salvation." He pointed out that "two of the spirits in the pre-existent world, known to us as Adam and Eve, should come upon the newly-formed earth, to become the parents of the human race." Adam and Eve stepped "down, as it were, to become subject to the conditions of earth. This [the fall] was the essence of the breaking of a law; but the necessary breaking of a lesser to conform to a higher law" (207). Widtsoe then elaborated on "The Place of Jesus Christ in the Plan" (208–9).

After the plan of salvation, in chapter 30, Widtsoe broached "Laws of Progression." This chapter discussed the basic gospel principles such as Law, Faith, Repentance, Baptism, and Obedience to Law (213–19). Chapter 31 essayed on the function and operation of the church within the plan of salvation. Widtsoe pointed out that "the Church is God's agency," designed to perform earthly ordinances and carry out God's purposes (220–22). In chapter 32, Widtsoe argued that salvation is universal, a doctrine unusual in Christianity, since many other churches believe in a division between Heaven and Hell. The bulk of the essay focuses on LDS temple ordinances for the dead (223–25). Widtsoe tackled the remainder of God's plan, especially resurrection and judgment in chapter 33, "Completion of the Plan" (226–31).

The final section of the book presents a summary of the beliefs and history of the church. Widtsoe began by listing the Articles of

Faith, then moved to a short overview of gospel dispensations, the "Falling Away," the Reformation, the church's founding, the settlement of the Mountain West, and recent church history (232–76).

Although Widtsoe continued his normal service as an apostle by conducting stake conferences and visiting missions, in some ways, *The Program of the Church of Jesus Christ of Latter-day Saints* (1936, 1937) was Widtsoe's most important achievement during his early years as an apostle, especially for the youth of the church. The book served as a text for the institutes of religion and for classes in the church's MIA.

In this volume, Widtsoe drew on both his scientific training and experience and religious faith and study to publish a book that encouraged Latter-day Saints to integrate secular and spiritual truths. Instead of going to an outside church-related publisher, Widtsoe turned to the Church Department of Education to publish this work. The book fit in well with the direction that church leaders had mapped out for its educational mission. With the exception of a few institutions, the church left secular education to the state and focused on religious education in seminaries, institutes, and the Mutual Improvement Association. Each of these religious organizations used his book for instruction. Under these circumstances, since the book carried the church's imprimatur, it opened the door for Latter-day Saints to follow Widtsoe's example of drawing on both scientific and religious insights to sustain their beliefs.

Moreover, although Widtsoe's tenure at the University of Southern California lasted only one academic year, its importance cannot easily be overstated. He brought the church's teachings to a world-renowned university while spreading the influence of an apostle to students and institutions in the Los Angeles area. Significantly, this outreach did not end when Widtsoe left USC. G. Homer Durham and Byron Done continued Widtsoe's work at USC and among LDS students in the Los Angeles area. Moreover, Durham married Widtsoe's daughter, Leah Eudora, and, in part, followed a career in higher education though in political science and university administration.

CHAPTER NINE

A RETURN TO IRRIGATION

Since Widtsoe had specialized in biochemical research on plants, soils, irrigation, and farming, the state and federal governments asked him to serve on boards and commissions that considered these subjects even after his call to be an LDS apostle. These included the Utah State Water Storage Board, the Utah Water and Power Board, a river expedition to examine the Colorado River for potential dam sites, assistance as an advisor and witness on the Colorado River Compact, and as vice president and secretary of the Fact Finding Commission to determine the fairness of US Bureau of Reclamation (BOR) irrigation project construction charges.[1]

On the recommendation of State Engineer R. E. Caldwell, Utah governor Charles R. Mabey appointed Widtsoe to the Utah State Water Storage Board. Widtsoe remained on the board under governors George H. Dern, Henry H. Blood, and Herbert B. Maw. The Water Storage Board dissolved in 1941, but in 1947 the legislature created the Utah Water and Power Board, and Maw appointed him to that agency as well. In 1925, Dern appointed Widtsoe to the Utah Water Storage Commission. In these positions, Widtsoe was an enthusiastic proponent of irrigation development.[2]

Until the years following World War II, the Green-Colorado River system was arguably Utah's most undeveloped source of potential water for irrigation and hydroelectric power. The Green-Colorado is the third largest drainage system in the United States after the

---

1. John A. Widtsoe, *In a Sunlit land, The Autobiography of John A. Widtsoe* (Salt Lake City: Milton R. Hunter and G. Homer Durham, 1952), 178; Alan K. Parrish, *John A. Widtsoe: A Biography* (Salt Lake City: Deseret Book Co., 2003), 339.

2. Widtsoe, *Sunlit Land*, 178.

Ohio-Missouri-Mississippi and the Snake-Columbia. In Utah, the Green-Colorado system drains the eastern slope of the Wasatch Mountains, the southern slope of the Uinta Mountains, and the eastern and southern slopes of Utah's portion of the Colorado Plateau.[3]

The Green River flows through southwestern Wyoming, enters Utah, then passes through eastern Colorado and into Utah again near Dinosaur National Monument. It draws water in all three states before joining the Colorado River, which enters Utah after originating in Colorado. The two rivers converge about sixty miles southwest of Moab on the Wayne County-San Juan County border. They drain some 40,000 acres in Utah; by 1920, they had irrigated some 359,000 acres of Utah lands. Because of the interest in developing water resources in the Colorado-Green system, the states of Utah, Wyoming, Colorado, New Mexico, Arizona, Nevada, and California, and the nation of Mexico had a vital interest in determining how much water each could use for irrigation and electric power and how they could control the rivers' rampaging floods.[4]

By 1920, Arthur Powell Davis, director of what was then called the US Reclamation Service, and which in 1923 was renamed the US Bureau of Reclamation, had concluded that the service would have to construct a large dam on the Colorado River to control floods and to facilitate irrigation and hydropower development. Floods on the river threatened farms in various states, including California's Imperial Valley. In addition, large areas accessible by river water were susceptible of irrigation, and the states expected hydroelectric power generated by dammed river water would help to pay for dam construction and operation.

In addition to locating dam sites on the Colorado River, a major barrier to the plans of the states and the federal government to develop the river's water resources lay in disputes over the ownership of the river's water. The laws regulating water rights generated some conflicts. With the exception of California, which had adopted both riparian rights and appropriation rights, the states of the Colorado

---

3. Norris Hundley Jr., *Water and the West: The Colorado River Compact and the Politics of Water in the American West* (Berkeley: University of California Press, 1975), 6, 7.

4. Hundley Jr., *Water and the West*, 141; DeLorme Mapping, *Utah Atlas & Gazetteer* (Freeport, ME: DeLorme Mapping, 1993), *passim*.

River basin had rejected riparian rights and legitimized appropriation to determine water rights. Appropriation meant that although the state owned the water, the first person to make beneficial use of the stream's water had the right to use it for as long as they did not abandon their claim. Under riparian law that existed, in part, in California and in all the states east of Colorado, every owner of land adjacent to a water course had the right to the stream's undiminished flow. Under California's hybrid system, water users could appropriate the water from a stream for a businesses, like irrigating or mining if they did so before another person owned land next to a stream. On the other hand, in California if someone owned land next to the water course, they held a riparian right to the stream's undiminished flow.[5]

Conflicts over appropriation arose both between users within the states, and between users in different states when streams flowed through two or more states. In the latter cases, the states themselves became parties to the disputes. Such disagreements affected the seven Colorado River states because the river or its tributaries flowed through each. As disputes over water ownership developed, each of the states watched clearly to see what happened to interstate water claims.

One such interstate disagreement arose over the Arkansas River, which originated in Colorado but flowed through Kansas as well. Kansas tried to claim all of the river's flow because it had legalized riparian rights, and it insisted that land owners adjacent to the river had a right to its undiminished flow. Since the river originated in Colorado, that state insisted on the right of its citizens to divert the river's waters under its appropriation doctrine. The dispute ended up in the US Supreme Court. In its 1907 *Kansas v. Colorado* decision, the court ruled that although the Arkansas River originated in Colorado and all of the water flowed from that state, and despite Kansas's riparian rights law, users in both states had an "equal right" to an "equitable apportionment" of the water since it flowed through both. Unfortunately, although the doctrine of "equitable apportionment" laid down by the court offered a guide to decisions in disputes over water rights,

---

5. For a discussion of this issue, see Hundley, *Water and the West*, 55–73; See also *Lux v. Hagan*, 69, California, 255 (1886).

it also resulted in interminable litigation because courts had to settle claims to equitable apportionment on their merits.[6]

Another conflict over an interstate stream arose between Wyoming and Colorado over the Laramie River, a tributary of the North Platte. Developers in Colorado proposed to divert a portion of the Laramie River into another drainage basin. This proposal created a dispute because when water remained in a river's basin, there was almost invariably some return flow that down-stream irrigators could tap for their use. Colorado insisted on diverting the water to a project in another basin using the equitable apportionment doctrine, but since none of the water diverted into another basin would have returned to the Laramie River, Wyoming argued that the appropriation of the Laramie River's waters in Wyoming took precedent. The dispute ended in the Supreme Court as *Wyoming* v. *Colorado* (1922).[7]

Unfortunately, the federal government threw a monkey wrench into what was already a fractious dispute. Attorneys from the US Attorney General's office insisted that the United States had authority over all the unappropriated waters in non-navigable streams in the West. The federal attorneys pointed out that the US had purchased the lands, and they said the national government had not surrendered to the states the right to use the surplus water of any of these streams that flowed from these lands. Accepting this assertion would have undermined the states' control of appropriation on all non-navigable waters in lands of the Louisiana Purchase, Mexican Cession, and Gadsden Purchase—virtually the entire area that had legalized appropriation.

Moreover, in addition to attempting to undermine state-regulated appropriation, the federal government threatened to assert control over the Green-Colorado system because it flowed through seven states and under the US Constitution the federal government could regulate interstate commerce. The federal government asserted this claim even though the courts had ruled that the streambed of a navigable stream belonged to the state in which it was situated.[8]

Fortunately, for Wyoming and Colorado and for all of the western

---

6. See Hundley, *Water and the West*, 73–76; and *Kansas* v. *Colorado* 206 U.S. 46 (1907).

7. *Wyoming* v. *Colorado*, 259 U.S. 419 (1922); Hundley, *Water and the West*, 76–78.

8. Hundley, *Water and the West*, 78–82.

states, the Supreme Court skirted the issue generated by the federal government's assertion of authority over the waters. The court ruled instead that since the states had "adopted and practised [appropriation] from the beginning with the sanction of the United States as owner of the public lands, and inasmuch as the United States does not now seek to impose any policy of its own choosing on either state, the question whether, in virtue of such ownership, it might do so, is not here considered." Instead, it ruled only on the dispute between Wyoming and Colorado. The court said that since both states had adopted appropriation, both had to recognize Wyoming's appropriation by allowing its appropriators to divert 272,500 acre-feet of an estimated 288,000 acre-feet in the stream's flow. Nevertheless, equitable apportionment also meant that Colorado developers could divert a small amount—15,500 acre feet—into another basin.[9]

The assertion of federal authority in *Wyoming v. Colorado* and the recognition that each of the states had an interest in settling the distribution of the water of the Green-Colorado system made necessary some solution to the ownership of the water in that system. In an ultimately successful attempt to resolve the distribution problem, Colorado attorney Delph Carpenter proposed that the seven Colorado basin states negotiate an interstate treaty as authorized in Article Six of the US Constitution. At a 1920 Denver meeting of representatives of the seven states, Carpenter convinced New Mexico state engineer Leslie W. Gillette to propose a conference of representatives of the seven states to negotiate an interstate compact on the waters of the Green-Colorado system. The states agreed to a confab because the lower basin states of California, Nevada, and Arizona wanted a dam at or near Boulder Canyon and the upper basin states of Wyoming, Colorado, Utah, and New Mexico wanted to protect their interests both in water and the revenue from hydropower generation.[10]

Delegates from the seven Colorado basin states met in Washington, DC, on January 26, 1922, but most of the negotiating occurred at Bishop's Lodge near Santa Fe, New Mexico. US President Warren Harding selected Commerce Secretary Herbert Hoover to chair the

9. *Wyoming v. Colorado*, 259 U.S. 419 (1922) at 465.
10. Hundley, *Water and the West*, 83–109, 133–37.

conference. Hoover had gained a positive reputation for humanitarianism as director of Belgium Relief during World War I and as an active promoter of interstate development while serving as commerce secretary. [11]

Although negotiations took place during the fall of 1922 in Bishop's Lodge, delegates held meetings earlier in the year throughout the seven-state area. Arthur Powell Davis had estimated that undistributed water from the Green-Colorado river system could irrigate an additional 456,000 acres in Utah. Utah's state engineer, R. E. Caldwell, thought Davis's estimates were too low and that Green-Colorado water could irrigate an additional 641,000 Utah acres. [12]

Because of Widtsoe's scientific studies of irrigation, Governor Mabey asked State Engineer Caldwell to induce Widtsoe to act as his principal advisor on the proposed compact. [13] Widtsoe had insisted that irrigation should take precedence over hydroelectric power and flood control as the most important aspect of Colorado River development. In March 1922, Widtsoe testified before the Interstate Commission. The lower basin states had already argued for a dam at or near Boulder Canyon. Widtsoe contended for a dam in Glen Canyon to facilitate irrigation in the upper basin states. In his testimony, Widtsoe elaborated on a theme that he had emphasized earlier in his career by arguing that agriculture constituted the basis of the region's future economic development. He cited Utah's nineteenth-century growth under Brigham Young's leadership in which the Saints settled in agricultural towns that provided the basis for future prosperity. Negotiators of the Colorado River Compact embodied part of Widtsoe's views in Section (b) of Article IV of the interstate agreement which said: "Subject to the provisions of this compact, water of the Colorado River System may be impounded and used for the generation of electrical power, but such impounding and use shall be subservient to the use and consumption of such water for agricultural and domestic purposes and shall not interfere with or prevent use for such dominant purposes." An article in the Santa Fe *New Mexican* on the conference congratulated Widtsoe for

11. Hundley, *Water and the West*, 138–39, 188–89.
12. Hundley, *Water and the West*, 147.
13. Widtsoe, *Sunlit Land*, 179; Hundley, *Water and the West*, 12–13.

his technical expertise and confirmed his role as the primary scientific advisor for the commission.[14]

Although representatives of the seven states signed the compact on November 24, 1922, the Arizona legislature refused to ratify it. The other six states, including Utah, ratified the compact and agreed to abide by it. The agreement required the upper basin states to deliver 7.5 million acre-feet to the lower basin at Lee's Ferry a point upstream from Grand Canyon. A subsequent 1948 Upper Basin Colorado River Compact gave Utah approximately 1.725 million acre feet of water per year of the upper basin's allocation of 7.5 million acre-feet. Following World War II, Arizona sued California over the distribution of lower basin water, and the US Supreme Court in *Arizona* v. *California* (1963) ruled that California should have 4.4 million acre feet and Arizona 2.8 million.[15]

The upper basin states needed to determine how they could deliver the water to the lower basin and allocate their portion for themselves. Although various people had conducted surveys of the Colorado River system, Davis believed that the Reclamation Service and the states needed additional information on upper basin dam sites. As the delegates from the seven Colorado basin states continued negotiations, Davis organized a survey in September 1922 to investigate part of the Colorado River "to see the results of the [previous] surveys." This was about six months after Widtsoe had testified before the Interstate Commission, and because of Widtsoe's expertise, Davis selected him as a member of the expedition. This expedition embarked at Hall's Landing and spent ten days floating down the Colorado to Lee's Ferry. In addition to locating a number of possible dam sites in Glen Canyon, where Widtsoe believed a dam was necessary for the upper basin states, Widtsoe commented on the wonders of the Colorado River gorge. As he floated down the river, he waxed eloquent about the romantic grandeur and scientific evidence he saw in the gorge that the river had spent millions of years etching through the Colorado plateau. The geologic landscape, the plant and animal life, and the results of human activity impressed him beyond imagination. As he viewed the canyon, he predicted that

14. Parrish, *Widtsoe*, 340–42.
15. *Arizona* v. *California*, 373 U.S. 546 (1963).

in the future people might enjoy a similar float trip to Lee's Ferry by traveling by auto to Hall's Landing. After floating to Lee's Ferry, Widtsoe's party traveled by train and car to the future site of Hoover Dam (initially called Boulder Dam). Construction on Hoover Dam did not begin, however, until 1931.[16]

After seeing his recommendation embodied in the Colorado River Compact and viewing the river gorge, Widtsoe had a further opportunity to consider the development of irrigation. By September 1923, the US government had sponsored reclamation projects throughout the west. These had been authorized under the Reclamation Projects or Newlands Act of 1902. In total, the government had constructed diversion projects that watered 6.3 percent of all irrigated lands in the nation. Unfortunately, by the early 1920s, a number of farmers on the projects had abandoned their holdings and nearly all of the remaining water users had fallen behind in their construction, operation, and management repayments to the government. Under those dire circumstances, US Secretary of the Interior Hubert Work decided to select a commission of citizens to investigate the projects and recommend solutions to the problem of repayment.[17]

As members of the commission, Widtsoe joined Thomas E. Campbell, former governor of Arizona; David W. Davis, who had replaced Arthur Powell Davis as Commissioner of Reclamation; Julius H. Barnes, president of the US Chamber of Commerce; Oscar E. Bradfute, president of the American Farm Bureau; James R. Garfield, former US Secretary of the Interior; and Elwood Mead, irrigation expert and professor at the University of California, Berkeley. Mead had to delay his participation because he was out of the country, and Barnes asked Clyde C. Dawson, an irrigation expert, to stand in for him. David Davis joined the commission but then resigned because he believed he could not fairly judge the repayment problems because of his position as BOR director.[18]

At their initial meeting in Washington, DC, on October 15, 1923, members of the so-called "Fact Finding Commission" chose

---

16. Widtsoe, *Sunlit Land*, 180.

17. Brian Q. Cannon, "'We Are Now Entering a New Era': Federal Reclamation and the Fact Finding Commission of 1923–1924," *Pacific Historical Review* 66 (May 1997): 185.

18. Cannon, "Fact Finding Commission," 186–87.

Campbell as chair and Widtsoe as vice-chair and secretary. They began their "Fact Finding" by interviewing Davis and Field Commissioner Miles Cannon about problems that precipitated the "poor repayment record." They discovered that only one of the BOR's twenty-eight projects had made "its payments on time." They learned also that farmers complained that they could not make their payments on time "or even at all." Under impossible pressure to meet the repayment schedule, some farmers talked seriously "about repudiating their debts." Unsympathetic with the farmers, Cannon and Davis argued that the bureau had been too lenient. Cannon said that the BOR had "demoralized" the settlers by failing to emphasize the importance of the repayments. Davis told the commissioners that the BOR should require mandatory repayments and institute monthly "interest penalties of two or three percent" if the settlers requested extensions. Utah Governor Charles Mabey disagreed. He pointed out that on Utah's Strawberry Valley project the farmers had been forced by circumstances to spend "fifty-eight percent of their gross annual income" on construction, operation, and maintenance of their irrigation system.[19]

As the commission continued its investigation, a number of members said that pressing obligations made it impossible to meet together regularly. As a stopgap, in order to continue their fact finding, commissioners deputized Campbell and Widtsoe to conduct daily sessions and to "present their findings" to the rest "of the members." Accepting this responsibility, Widtsoe drew up a plan for the two of them. They were to consider "planning and development, engineering structures, soil, climate, drainage, markets," transportation, settlement, and land disposition on each project. To understand the settlers on the projects, the two agreed to investigate the settlers' socioeconomic background, financial performance, and standard of living together with the socioeconomic institutions available on each project. The two proposed also to investigate the economic and agricultural conditions on each project by determining their "cropping patterns, irrigation practices, agricultural productivity," operation costs, "project management, and relations between the settlers" and the BOR.[20]

19. Cannon, "Fact Finding Commission," 188–90.
20. Cannon, "Fact Finding Commission," 190.

To understand the relationship of the BOR with the farmers, Widtsoe and Campbell investigated the operation and management of the BOR. How much did the agency invest, why was the cost of constructing the projects so much in excess of the amount the bureau had estimated it would cost, and the bottom line: Were the settlers really able to repay the government? A report by Secretary Work showed that construction costs on the BOR projects had generated overruns "2.7 times greater than" the original estimates, and if the BOR considered only the lands actually irrigated in 1922, they ran to four times the original estimate. They also learned that in total, the farmers had repaid "only two-thirds of the expense of operating the projects," and "only eleven percent" of the construction cost.[21]

Widtsoe and Campbell met with various experts and undertook an exhaustive examination of previous records. They examined reports of the BOR, reports of the department's Board of Review, testimony of project farmers, reports by special agents of the BOR and US Interior Department, and documents from previous investigations. They listened to testimony from "agricultural experts, economists, accountants, politicians," and others. They found that in some cases, during construction and operation engineers and contractors refused to accommodate the farmers even on "minor issues." They insisted on doing things their own way although they "knew little about irrigation or … farming." Frederick Haynes Newell, former Reclamation Service director, testified that the Reclamation Act and political pressure led to building projects in relation to "the volume of public land sales in various states," and that some of those who complained at the cost of construction were speculators who "owned more land than they could farm."[22]

In late November 1923, Widtsoe and Campbell reported on their exhaustive investigation to the other commission members. They did so under the pressure of conflicting and contentious recommendations from politicians and the bureau. These included differences of opinion on the repayment plan. Should the farmers repay only the original construction estimate? Should the BOR institute "mandatory repayment schedules?" Should the farmers pay double or triple

---

21. Cannon, "Fact Finding Commission," 190, 192.
22. Cannon, "Fact Finding Commission," 191–92.

interest penalties, and should these apply to all settlers? The BOR thought such penalties would induce speculators to sell their excess holdings. Should the farmers float bonds to repay the government? Should the government extend the repayment period to twenty or forty years instead of the current ten, and should it impose a moratorium of two to five years on the repayments?[23]

The commissioners considered each of the recommendations, but they thought that the proposals lacked a consideration of "the productivity of each farm." The commissioners decided that they needed to classify soils on each farm by its productivity and income. They concluded that if they made such calculations, well-to-do farmers and speculators "could no longer evade payments."[24]

To assist in calculating various repayment schedules, the commissioners met with F. W. Schmitt of the *Engineering News Record*. Schmitt had investigated nine bureau projects, and he believed that farmers on poorer soils should have a longer time to repay construction costs. He pointed out, nevertheless, that some farmers had brought the debt burden on themselves by mortgaging their farms to speculate in oil stocks. As a whole, Schmitt believed, "any reasonably good farmer" could support his family and repay the construction and operation costs.[25]

As Christmas 1923 approached, Widtsoe became discouraged over the length of time the investigation had consumed, and he wrote his friend Francis W. Kirkham that the investigation was "dragging out longer than I expected." Earlier in the month, Widtsoe, Campbell, and Garfield agreed to draft a report by the end of 1923. That deadline came and went, and by early January 1924 they had still not finished their report. Before Christmas they had planned to visit a number of projects in January 1924 because they believed such visits necessary to understand the problems that the settlers had encountered. They concluded, however, that such visits would take at least two months, and they had come under increasing pressure to finish their report. Instead of making the project visits, the commissioners invited each project to send delegates to a conference in Salt Lake City.[26]

---

23. Cannon, "Fact Finding Commission," 192–93.
24. Cannon, "Fact Finding Commission," 193–94.
25. Cannon, "Fact Finding Commission," 193.
26. Cannon, "Fact Finding Commission," 194.

Commissioners and representatives of all the projects except two met in Salt Lake City's Hotel Utah on January 17, 1924. Representing the committee, Widtsoe, Campbell, Garfield, and Mead met 175 delegates at the opening session. They listened to testimony that, when transcribed, filled 1,764 pages of text, and they collected additional documents, including surveys and water user affidavits. Some of the delegates orated in lengthy and flowery speeches. Disappointed at such filibustering, Campbell cut them short, telling them to "get down to brass tacks." Some of the delegates pointed to the decline in crop prices and bank failures that had occurred during an economic recession that occurred from 1919 to 1922. Many delegates requested that the government "extend the repayment period," as it had previously done. William Treiber of the Minidoka Project in Idaho said that if the government "could give its European allies thirty to sixty years to repay their war debts ... 'we ought to get as much consideration.'" In a seeming but obvious non-sequitur, the delegates asked for debt relief while asking for additional appropriations to complete the projects that would irrigate their farms.[27]

The water users who testified generally complained about the way the government treated them. One representative pointed out that the construction costs had inflated 300 percent; another expressed displeasure that the BOR had threatened to cut off their water for delinquent payments. Under questioning from Widtsoe, the latter representative admitted that in spite of the threat, the water had not been cut off. A number of farmers wanted to take over management of the dams and ditches themselves instead of the current practice in which the BOR managed the project then charged farmers for the service. Some maintained that management charges were too high.[28]

Not all water users had fallen into dire straits. Some were making money on their farms, and others had sufficient land they could lease out their farms to tenants. In some cases, affluent farmers from some projects dominated the delegations that came to the Salt Lake conference. In others cases, farmers could not agree with each other.

---

27. Cannon, "Fact Finding Commission," 195–96.
28. Cannon, "Fact Finding Commission," 197.

On the Boise Project in Idaho, they had actually split into two competing water users' associations.[29]

Because of other commitments, some of the delegates left the hearings before they were over. After listening to delegates from a large number of projects, Campbell asked those who remained to organize into a Federated Reclamation Water Users Association. The delegates elected a president and met to draft several resolutions to apply to all the projects. The resolutions "guided the Fact Finding Commission in preparing its ... recommendations."[30]

The report and recommendations of the commission that Mead, Campbell, Garfield, and Widtsoe played the most important role in drafting included some recommendations for changes in Bureau of Reclamation policy and proposals for congressional legislation. The recommendations included: granting temporary relief to settlers; not undertaking projects and extensions of projects without an expert investigation; estimating the cost of projects more carefully; allocating costs to farmers on the productivity of the land; classifying the physical and economic value of the land; not charging construction costs for infertile land; stressing that in the future the bureau should select settlers for "industry, experience, character, and capital"; urging settlers to form irrigation districts and take over management of the projects; using credit income from power plants to cover construction costs; setting penalties for unpaid charges at 6 percent rather than the current 12 percent; making payment plans more flexible; asking authorities to cooperate with the Department of Agriculture and agricultural experiment stations to disseminate information on crops and methods of farming best suited for various types of land on each project; requiring the owners of four projects to sell excess land at prices the secretary of the interior determines; reducing the rental charge on the Lower Yellowstone project in Montana because of unwarranted and excessive costs; and not charging the costs of general investigation of projects to construction costs.[31]

---

29. Cannon, "Fact Finding Commission," 198.
30. Cannon, "Fact Finding Commission," 198.
31. Paul W. Gates, *History of Public Land Law Development* (Washington, DC: Public Land Law Review Commission, 1968), 676–77.

The commission also recommended the reorganization of the BOR into three divisions: engineering to undertake construction, operation, and maintenance; finance to supervise expenditures and collections; and farm economics to assist the farmers in planning and improving farm practices, to classify land, and to promote settlement.[32]

Congress attached many of the recommendations of the Fact Finding Commission to a deficiency appropriation act in December 1924. The provisions attached to the act were generally called the Fact Finders' Act. The Fact Finders' Act placed a moratorium on new projects until the BOR had gained accurate information on costs, water supply, and the viability of a proposed project. In the future, the act required the BOR to determine the suitability of the applicants, classify the lands according to potential productivity, and levy charges on the basis of five percent of the gross acreage income rather than as a fixed amount. Furthermore, the BOR had to make annual reports to Congress on physical problems that made repayment of construction cost impossible, and was prohibited from charging Washington Office costs to project construction, operation, or maintenance.[33]

Because of his understanding of irrigation and farmers' needs, Widtsoe provided both Utah and the nation with valuable services. As a member of various Utah state boards, he offered advice that the state was able to use in implementing policy. As a member of the float trip to examine Glen Canyon and the middle Colorado River, he helped to lay the ground work for the construction of Glen Canyon Dam. The media and the commission recognized his service as the principal advisor during the discussions of the Colorado River compact. He was particularly influential in inducing the negotiators to classify irrigation as the principal goal of the compact. Although many of the members of the Fact Finding Commission could not remain during the full time the members took testimony, examined documents, and drafted their report, Widtsoe was one of the few who did. This was an arduous and time-consuming responsibility, but with his usual tenacity, Widtsoe stayed to the end. The work he and the few others who remained laid the groundwork for the Fact

32. Gates, *History of Public Land Law*, 677.
33. Gates, *History of Public Land Law*, 677–78.

Finders' Act and the restructuring of Bureau of Reclamation policy and practice for future years.

CHAPTER TEN

RETURNING TO EUROPE
AS MISSION PRESIDENT

During the 1910s and 1920s, the LDS Church, its leadership, its members, and its missionary force experienced extreme difficulty to carry on normal religious activities and to preach the gospel throughout the world. World War I broke out in Europe in 1914, and in 1917 the United States joined the war on the side of the Allies: England, France, Russia, Finland, and Italy in their fight against Germany and Austria-Hungary. As the war began, Apostle George F. Richards presided over the European Mission with headquarters in Liverpool. He remained in England and continued to serve throughout the war. Since American missionaries could not travel to the United Kingdom, in order to continue church work, Richards appointed local members to fill posts in the missions in Great Britain and Ireland. Strapped for men, most of whom had been called to serve in the military, Richards called women to officiate—a function usually reserved for priesthood-holding men—in local auxiliary organizations such as Sunday school and YMMIA. He also assigned women to do branch teaching, a task equivalent to what was then called ward teaching in organized wards. Significantly, in spite of the absence of American missionaries and British men, attendance at branch services, payment of tithes, and baptisms actually increased during 1917 over comparative numbers in 1915 and 1916.[1]

After Armistice ended the war in November 1918, the British government still declined to provide visas for missionaries to enter

---

1. George F. Richards, Journal, June 15, Nov. 19, Dec. 5, 1916, Jan. 10, Mar. 1, 1918, Sep. 1918, Church History Library, Church of Jesus Christ of Latter-day Saints, Salt Lake City, Utah.

the United Kingdom, Australia, and New Zealand.[2] As mission president, Richards pled with the British labor minister to secure the revocation of the order that denied landing permits for missionaries. The minister finally relented, and on June 6, 1919, the first LDS missionaries entered the country, but only with conditional permission.[3]

In an attempt to facilitate missionary work on the continent, in May 1919 Richards tried to tour the western European countries. National governments allowed him to enter the Netherlands and France, but the Swiss government refused entrance.[4]

Church leaders turned to the embassies of European governments in Washington, DC, to open their borders to church representatives. Serving in Washington as US Senator from Utah, Apostle Reed Smoot, accompanied by George Albert Smith of the Quorum of the Twelve Apostles, met with representatives of England to secure permission for missionaries to enter the country and to allow a new mission president travel to Great Britain to replace George Richards. The British government extended, revoked, then finally granted such permission.[5]

Unfortunately, as missionaries began to return to the United Kingdom, anti-Mormon activity accelerated. Throughout August 1919, the British press conducted a campaign of anti-Mormon propaganda. In spite of the formal action against new plural marriages that the church conducted after 1904, newspapers continued to claim that Mormon missionaries had come to Britain to induce young women to become polygamous wives. In Washington, Smoot implored UK embassy officials to allow the missionaries unrestricted entry to Great Britain and the commonwealth countries. He finally secured permanent permission in June 1920.[6]

---

2. Joseph F. Smith, "Review of Church's Condition—Peace" *Improvement Era*, 18 (Nov. 1914): 74–75; Joseph F. Smith to Reed Smoot, June 23, 1917, James R. Clark, *Messages of the First Presidency ...*, vol. 5 (Salt Lake City: Bookcraft, 1971) 78; Deseret News, *Church Almanac, 1974*, 198.

3. Richards Journal, June 6, 12, 1919.

4. Richards Journal, May 7, 31, June 5, 6, 12, 1919.

5. Reed Smoot, Diary, May 8, 1919, L. Tom Perry Special Collections, Harold B. Lee Library, Brigham Young University, Provo, Utah; see also Harvard S. Heath, ed., *In the World: The Diaries of Reed Smoot* (Salt Lake City: Signature Books, 1997), 415.

6. Journal History of the Church of Jesus Christ of Latter-day Saints, Church History Library, Aug. 31, 1919; Smoot, Diary, May 8, Sep. 20, 25, 1919, June 15, 1920; Heath, *In the World*, 415, 420, 443.

Smoot also worked assiduously with the legations of Holland, Switzerland, Denmark, Norway, Sweden, and Germany to allow missionaries entrance. In May 1920 he convinced the Netherlands to allow missionaries to enter. In December 1920, he secured permission for missionaries to reenter Germany. In 1921, Smoot obtained entry permission from Sweden, Norway, Denmark, Switzerland, Holland, and South Africa, but only for restricted access. Each missionary had to secure an individual visa for each entry. In April 1921, however, Sweden rescinded the permission it had previously granted.[7]

Vocal and violent anti-Mormon campaigns accompanied the anti-Mormon newspaper wars and the struggle to obtain entry to foreign countries. During January 1922 and afterward in England, various anti-Mormons, especially Protestant ministers, issued challenges to missionaries for debates. Debates were one thing, but anti-Mormon mob violence occurred in Plymouth and other cities in February and March 1922. In June 1922, a gang of Edinburgh University students raided the local Latter-day Saint meetinghouse and assaulted two elderly Saints. In June 1924, the British press falsely alleged that church agents had abducted a British girl. As these events unfolded in England, missionaries encountered opposition in Scandinavian countries, and they found it difficult to gain entry to any of the Nordic areas.[8]

Because of the pervasive anti-Mormon sentiment throughout Europe, the church faced massive odds to reverse the efforts to prevent missionaries from laboring in various countries and to allow the church members to continue normal religious activities anywhere. In 1920 and 1921, Elders David O. McKay of the Twelve and Hugh J. Cannon, president of the Liberty Stake (Salt Lake City), made a tour around the world to spread good will. After McKay returned to the United States, in November 1922 church president Heber J. Grant called him to serve as European Mission president. Like previous mission presidents, he was stationed in Liverpool.[9]

---

7. Journal History, Aug. 31, 1919; May 3, 13, 1920; Smoot Diary, May 8, Sep. 20, 25, 1919, June 15, 1920; Heath, *In the World*, 419, 437–38.

8. Journal History, Jan. 28, Feb. 23, Mar. 8, June 18, 1922, June 26, 1924; John A. Widtsoe, *In a Sunlit Land: The Autobiography of John A. Widtsoe* (Salt Lake City: Milton R. Hunter and G. Homer Durham, 1952), 186.

9. Heber J. Grant, Diary, Nov. 4, 1922, Church History Library.

As the anti-Mormon campaign continued to accelerate and church members and missionaries encountered press and public opposition, the First Presidency sent Reed Smoot and John Widtsoe to Europe to try to overcome or at least mitigate the opposition. As Widtsoe put it, "Enemies of the Church, chiefly ministers were industriously circulating untruths about us." The choice of Widtsoe was particularly fortuitous because he spoke several European languages in addition to Norwegian, his native language, and German, where he had studied.[10]

Sailing from New York on the maiden voyage of the *Leviathan*, Smoot and Widtsoe landed in England and went immediately to London to meet with British officials and newspaper publishers. They met with newspaper owners, including Lord Beaverbrook, of the London *Express*, *Evening Standard*, and the Glasgow *Evening Citizen*. They also met with a number of officials, including former prime minister Stanley Baldwin. The information that Smoot provided on the church led the newspaper owners to understand "that they had been printing rot." After speaking with Smoot, newspaper representatives "agreed ... henceforth would no longer accept anti-Mormon material." Widtsoe believed that after this agreement "persecution largely disappeared" during the 1920s. Nevertheless, some anti-Mormon gatherings occurred in England as late as 1929.[11]

After visiting the United Kingdom, Smoot and Widtsoe traveled to the continent. Like Widtsoe, Smoot's mother, Kristine Mauritzdatter, had been born in Norway. So, in addition to contacting government officials, they visited Smoot's mother's childhood home. There they found a family Bible with his mother's farewell message to her family, written in Norwegian. Widtsoe translated the message for Smoot. It contained her thoughts about the rewards of joining Christ's church and her hope that the remainder of her family would convert to the Church of Jesus Christ of Latter-day Saints. She called upon everyone to repent and prepare for Christ's second coming.[12]

---

10. Widtsoe, *Sunlit Land*, 186.

11. Widtsoe, *Sunlit Land*, 187; Thomas G. Alexander, *Mormonism in Transition: A History of the Latter-day Saints, 1890–1930* (3rd ed.; Salt Lake City: Greg Kofford Books, 2012), 243.

12. Widtsoe, *Sunlit Land*, 187–88.

In Stockholm, Widtsoe searched for books on Swedish genealogy. He felt a premonition to turn down the "rather narrow side
street." There he found an obscure store with a large collection of
genealogical books. The bookstore "had bought the library of one of
the foremost collectors of books on Swedish genealogy." Although
the collection was expensive, Widtsoe bought it for the LDS Family
History Library.[13]

In the wake of Smoot's and Widtsoe's visit, during the 1920s
the church opened or reopened several missions. Widtsoe credited
the change to "Smoot's visit," but Widtsoe was partly responsible
as well. The French allowed them to reopen their mission in 1923,
the German-Austrian mission reopened in 1925, and Widtsoe was
instrumental in opening a mission in Czechoslovakia in 1929. The
mission in Germany remained open in spite of some opposition they
encountered in 1924 from Bavaria's predominantly Catholic population. The most intense opposition to mission activities, however,
developed among Catholics in Czechoslovakia where several people
entered lawsuits against the missionaries.[14]

In November 1927, church leaders called Widtsoe to return again
to Europe to preside over the European and British missions. His
wife, Leah, and their youngest daughter, Eudora, accompanied him.
He occupied the same mission home in which previous presidents
had resided in Liverpool.[15]

After he arrived in England, Widtsoe and the church's First Presidency decided that they should open a mission in Czechoslovakia.
After the breakup of the Austro-Hungarian Empire following World
War I, Czechoslovakia had organized a democratic government under the leadership of Tomáš Masaryk. LDS leaders believed they
might find a degree of religious freedom because of the new emphasis on democracy. They also expected that by opening this Slavic
country, they might open a gateway to the Soviet Union despite the
October Revolution in 1917 that had led to the installation of an
atheistic Communist government. The First Presidency decided to

---

13. Widtsoe, *Sunlit Land*, 188–89.
14. Journal History, Mar. 17, May 31, 1927, Sep. 20, 1928, May 10, 26, 1929; Smoot
Diary, Aug. 3, 1928; Widtsoe, *Sunlit Land*, 189.
15. Widtsoe, *Sunlit Land*, 189–90.

call Arthur Gaeth, who had presided over the German mission and who was married to Martha K. Gaeth, a Czech-American. Mrs. Gaeth had some influential friends in Prague, and LDS leaders believed that these relationships might assist with missionary activity. To accompany Gaeth in opening the mission, the church selected half dozen elders then serving in Germany. On July 24, 1929, a group of Latter-day Saints, including Widtsoe and German-Austrian Mission president H. W. Valentine, met near Karlstein Castle and dedicated the land for missionary work.[16]

Widtsoe and Gaeth began their work by visiting "national leaders and representatives of the public press." The meetings with opinion makers proved prescient because the Catholic Church did not approve of the Latter-day Saints. The Catholics went as far as entering a lawsuit against the church. Because the LDS leaders had developed friendships with national leaders, the suit "came to naught."[17]

Widtsoe initiated a number of changes in addition to opening the mission in Czechoslovakia that helped to facilitate proselytizing in Europe. Since the organization of missions on the European Continent, the president of the British Mission had served concurrently as European Mission president. Moreover, when Widtsoe arrived in Europe, the dual mission president had no counselors in either capacity. This dual-presidency created a burden for the president. Since there were no stakes in the United Kingdom at the time, and because he served as president of the British Mission and was the only LDS general authority in Great Britain, Widtsoe had to attend district conferences in the United Kingdom forty Sundays each year. In addition, as European Mission president, he had to visit all eleven missions in Europe one or more times each year. He also organized a conference of the eleven mission presidents in Europe once each year.[18]

To take some of the burden from the shoulders of the combined presidency, Widtsoe recommended that the church leadership call counselors for mission presidents and that they call a separate president for the British Mission. The First Presidency and Quorum of

---

16. Widtsoe, *Sunlit Land*, 190–91.
17. Widtsoe, *Sunlit Land*, 191.
18. Widtsoe, *Sunlit Land*, 192–93.

the Twelve agreed to both proposals. The First Presidency called A. William Lund, a son of Anthon H. Lund (late first counselor in the First Presidency), as British Mission president and his wife, Sarah Ann Peterson Lund, to accompany him. The First Presidency also approved Widtsoe's request to call counselors.[19]

After receiving approval, Widtsoe selected two counselors for himself and had the other eleven European mission presidents do the same. He made some other changes in the interest of unity in the missions. Each of the missions had been providing unique lesson materials for their auxiliaries and classes. Widtsoe believed this practice presented a problem since it made the church different in each country. To offer a degree of uniformity among the missions, Widtsoe obtained documents for the various classes the church had published in America. He revised them to meet the cultural needs of the various European countries, republished them, and distributed them to the missions. He asked the various missions to use these uniform materials rather than those published locally. His wife, Leah, assisted in the project by adapting materials from church headquarters for the Relief Society and MIA. Widtsoe and his wife took three years of research and writing to complete the lesson manuals, but they considered this a necessary task. When the two visited Salt Lake City to attend general conference in 1931, they consulted with the various boards about their project, and received the boards' full cooperation.[20]

Before Widtsoe became European Mission president, the other mission presidents had met together with the European president at irregular times. Widtsoe believed it was important that the presidents hold a conference together at least annually to receive instruction and coordinate their efforts. To accomplish those goals, he instituted an annual European mission president's conference. They met the first time with Widtsoe at a house in Meudon, a suburban municipality 9.1 km southwest of Paris. While the presidents met with Widtsoe, Leah held a separate meeting for their wives. At the time, in most of the missions the wives of the presidents served as mission Relief Society president, and Leah organized a program to

19. Widtsoe, *Sunlit Land*, 191–92.
20. Widtsoe, *Sunlit Land*, 192–93.

help them carry out their responsibilities in that position.[21] Under Widtsoe's direction, the presidents held subsequent conferences in Liverpool, Basel, Frankfurt, Prague, and Copenhagen.[22]

As the presidents gathered for the conference in Meudon, a number of reporters came to interview them. Since the interviews reflected positively on the proselytizing work and on the beliefs and activities of the church, Widtsoe published them in French as a tract. He believed that the published interviews helped to break down prejudice against the church. Anything that could counteract the negative publicity about the church was sorely needed. During the 1930s and well into the mid-twentieth century, many in Europe still believed that church members were marrying in new polygamous relationships and that the missionaries had come to Europe to persuade, or even trick, young women to join the church to marry as polygamous wives.[23]

As supplements to the interviews tract, Widtsoe believed that the church needed additional tracts for missionaries to distribute in Europe. Since most people no longer read the Bible, he reasoned that the missionaries could not teach LDS doctrines and practices from the scriptures alone. He decided that instead of just reissuing older tracts, the missionaries needed new tracts. In some countries, like England, missionaries had been active so long that most people knew about the tracts the church distributed. To gain information about the type of tracts the missionaries needed, Widtsoe sent a questionnaire to the missionaries in Europe.[24]

After tabulating the results of the questionnaire, Widtsoe took three weeks from his ordinary duties to write "a series of tracts," which he called the *Centennial Series*. He chose that title because he published them in 1930, the church's centennial. By the period shortly before his death in 1952, Widtsoe knew that the *Centennial* tracts had been widely circulated.[25]

---

21. Widtsoe, *Sunlit Land*, 193.
22. Widtsoe, *Sunlit Land*, 194.
23. Widtsoe, *Sunlit Land*, 193–94. During the time I served an LDS proselytizing mission in Germany from 1956 to 1958, many people still believed that church members practiced polygamy.
24. Widtsoe, *Sunlit Land*, 194.
25. Widtsoe, *Sunlit Land*, 194.

To supplement the *Centennial Series,* Widtsoe also authorized the use of other books and tracts. He approved and introduced Franklin S. Harris's book, *Seven Claims of the Book of Mormon,* and a series of small tracts, including *The Successful Missionary, Studies in Priesthood, What Is Mormonism?,* and *What Others Say.*

To improve the proselytizing work, Widtsoe asked the First Presidency to call women to serve as missionaries. In addition to proselytizing, he believed that the missions needed women to "lead out in Primary, Y.W.M.I.A., and Relief Society." He considered it too burdensome to expect the mission president's wife to run a large home, entertain missionaries, visiting authorities, and dignitaries, and to preside concurrently without counselors over the women's auxiliaries. Widtsoe sent many letters arguing his case for women missionaries before the First Presidency agreed. They called two women, Nettie Woodbury and Ileen Ann Waspe, as the first sister missionaries to serve in Europe in at least thirty-five years. The two were such excellent missionaries that the First Presidency called additional women. Women served in Europe until World War II broke out.[26]

For many years, the church had assigned missionaries to serve as branch presidents and in other leadership positions in branches and districts. The callings gave missionaries "good experience," but it denied local priesthood holders the responsibility and training necessary to grow in church experience. In addition, while serving as branch presidents, the missionaries had to carry out various administrative duties, which reduced the time they could proselytize and share the gospel with others. Often those who favored the practice of calling missionaries to such positions argued that in small branches members tended to become jealous of those called to such positions and would not support the leaders. Widtsoe believed that if such were the case, calling a missionary to these positions offered only a temporary palliative. If a missionary presided for a long period of time, he could also become a target for the disaffected. In addition, missionaries served only two or two-and-a-half years, and since some were constantly coming and going, the president had to transfer them in order to provide assignments for the new

---

26. Widtsoe, *Sunlit Land,* 195.

missionaries and replace those who were released. Thus, as soon as a missionary became acquainted with branch members and learned of any problems in the branch, it was possible, even likely, that he would be transferred or released.[27]

Since Widtsoe was a European by birth, he knew of the capability of those from the eastern side of the Atlantic Ocean, and he began as much as possible to train and call local members to responsible positions in priesthood and auxiliary positions. In most cases, he considered "the results ... remarkable." He trained leaders to understand the limits of their authority. He called Europeans to serve in branch, district, and mission-wide positions. As soon as he could, he called his wife to serve as general supervisor of women's work rather than as mission-wide Relief Society president. In place of Leah, he called local women, or when they were unavailable, sister missionaries to serve as presidents and counselors in women's organizations. One advantage of Widtsoe's decision to call local leaders was that during World War II, the church could continue to function even though American missionaries could not travel to Europe. In those instances where local men and women had been called to positions, they had already been trained to carry out their responsibilities.[28]

After Widtsoe arrived in Europe, he noted that subjects of the United Kingdom often experienced poor health. Many lost their teeth early in life, and they suffered from other diseases resulting from poor nutrition. Some of the poor nutrition may have resulted from shortages during World War I. Some may have resulted from insufficient income. In other cases, however, many people simply did not know much about good nutrition. Widtsoe could not do much about the general British population, but he could work on the problem with church members. Leah, whose background and education gave her the expertise to begin dealing with problems of nutrition, volunteered to assist. Widtsoe encouraged her to do so, and she began a campaign to improve the health of the British members. She prepared a series of lessons on the positive aspects of the Word of Wisdom as outlined in Doctrine and Covenants 89. In both Europe and the United States, most members considered the Word

---

27. Widtsoe, *Sunlit Land*, 195–96.
28. Widtsoe, *Sunlit Land*, 196–97.

of Wisdom to consist of avoiding alcohol, tobacco, tea, and coffee. Often, they paid little attention to the healthful foods mentioned in the scripture. Leah Widtsoe's campaign produced positive results. President Widtsoe wrote, "Scores testified to the benefit received ... telling about relief from pain and suffering, and the actual cure of diseases suffered for years." Widtsoe firmly believed that the church "must ever try to care for the whole man."[29]

When Widtsoe landed in Liverpool in 1927 to take his place as European and British Mission president, the church had sent him, as they did other mission presidents and missionaries, by a Canadian line. In 1928, the church switched to the U.S. Lines, and they docked in Southampton or Plymouth. After they disembarked, missionaries traveled by boat train to London and went from there to their various fields of labor. At the time, the European Mission headquarters was located in Durham House in Liverpool. Because of the travel arrangements, the European Mission president seldom met the new missionaries. Unfortunately, Liverpool's Durham House had deteriorated because of insufficient funds to make the necessary repairs. When Widtsoe arrived in England, he learned that to make the home and headquarters in Liverpool serviceable, he would need to spend a large amount of money. Since he would prefer to have headquarters near the British Mission office and the place where the missionaries left for their fields of labor, Widtsoe recommended that the church move European Mission headquarters to London.[30]

The church leadership approved this proposal, and Widtsoe found headquarters for the European Mission and an apartment for his family near the British Museum and close to the headquarters of the British Mission. John and Leah frequently invited missionaries living in London, those passing through the city, and visitors to the city to come to their apartment for a social gathering on Saturday evening. They also invited "people of influence," who were not Latter-day Saints, to visit or to eat dinner with them. After moving the mission office to London, Widtsoe encouraged the office staff to rent lodging with non-members in apartments nearby. Since the

---

29. Widtsoe *Sunlit Land*, 197–98.
30. Widtsoe, *Sunlit Land*, 198–99.

staff worked in the office during the day, they were free to proselytize in London during the evening.[31]

Leah initiated the visit of one of England's most prominent personalities. She learned that the noted Irish playwright and novelist George Bernard Shaw, who was living in London, had spoken favorably about Brigham Young, her grandfather. In 1930, Leah and her mother, Susa Young Gates, had co-authored and published *The Life Story of Brigham Young* with Jarrolds, a prominent British publisher. Leah wrote to Shaw, telling him about the book and inviting him to come to the mission headquarters to secure a copy. She thought it unlikely that Shaw would respond, but to their surprise, he showed up at the mission headquarters. Leah gave him a copy of the book and invited him to dinner. Shaw countered that instead of coming to their apartment, the Widtsoes should have dinner with him in his home. They accepted, and visiting in his elegant mansion, they learned that Shaw did not want to know how many members they had in Great Britain, but rather "how many of your converts do you keep." That, to him, was most pertinent, and Widtsoe thought the question "one of the important things" church leaders had to "keep in mind."[32]

In 1932, while Widtsoe was serving in England, church leaders asked him to travel to Aleppo, Syria, to dedicate the grave of Joseph W. Booth, who had died there while serving as Turkish Mission president. While in Asia Minor, Widtsoe was also to install Badwagan Piranian as president of the Palestine-Syrian Mission with headquarters in Haifa. The Widtsoe party traveled through Italy, then by ship to Alexandria. They spent a week in Cairo where they visited the "museum, the sphinx, pyramids ..."[33]

Through the good offices of American Minister to Egypt, William M. Jardine, who had studied with Widtsoe at USAC, Widtsoe took a trip on the Nile. Widtsoe was particularly interested in irrigation projects in the area that he saw in passing. The Widtsoe party met with a number of important Egyptian officials. Some of them had studied in France where the professors used "some of" Widtsoe's books on irrigation as texts.[34]

---

31. Widtsoe, *Sunlit Land*, 199.
32. Widtsoe, *Sunlit Land*, 200–1.
33. Widtsoe, *Sunlit Land*, 207.
34. Widtsoe, *Sunlit Land*, 207.

After touring in Egypt, Widtsoe's party traveled by train and car through Palestine and Syria. They visited small congregations of members in Haifa and Damascus. Widtsoe noted with interest the fields and orchards in the Jezreel Valley of Palestine and the biblical sites of Nazareth, Cana, and the Sea of Galilee. The party drove west from Damascus to Beirut, where they also conversed with members. From there, they motored north through Tripoli to Antioch and to Aleppo. Joseph Wilford Booth had been buried in a cemetery outside Aleppo. On June 18, 1933, Widtsoe dedicated Booth's grave in a service attended by a number of members.[35]

Most church members in the Middle East were Armenians who had been traditional Christians. A few Arabs and other Muslims joined. Members in the area met together in small branches. In spite of the paucity of members and the lack of contact with church headquarters, Widtsoe noted that they conducted their church services and carried out their responsibilities.[36]

Throughout his travels in Palestine, Syria, Lebanon, and Turkey, Widtsoe commented on small villages and famous biblical archaeological sites. He saw piles of camel dung dried for winter heating, and he noted, as may be expected, the irrigation projects. In some areas, he saw pumps drawing water from as much as 2,000 feet deep. In one of the villages, Widtsoe conversed with a twelve-year-old girl who had been born in Boston and who spoke English. He marveled at the immense stones that graced the ruins of Baalbek where Solomon was said to have built a palace for his Egyptian queen. In the mountains, he saw the famous cedars of Lebanon of the type used in building Solomon's temple and contemporary terraced landscapes on which Arabs farmed.[37]

After dedicating Booth's grave near Aleppo and visiting members, Widtsoe and his party returned to Haifa. The church had established its headquarters in that city, which had become an important seaport. He noted Mount Carmel south of Haifa on which Elijah challenged priests of Baal to a contest over the power of their

---

35. Widtsoe, *Sunlit Land*, 208–10.
36. Widtsoe, *Sunlit Land*, 208.
37. Widtsoe, *Sunlit Land*, 209.

129

gods, which Yahveh won. In Haifa, Widtsoe negotiated to have the Book of Mormon published in Hebrew.[38]

From Haifa, John and Leah traveled to Tel Aviv, a Mediterranean city inhabited entirely by Jews. In Tel Aviv, among other things, the Widtsoes celebrated their thirty-fifth wedding anniversary. They expected to enjoy a well-deserved rest, but Eliezer Volcani, who directed agricultural activity for the Jewish people in Palestine, read of their presence and contacted John. Through Volcani, John learned of the agricultural work particularly at the kibbutzim the Jews had established in the Holy Land. The Widtsoes attended a conference of authors writing in "modern Hebrew," and they stopped at hospitals and schools. They visited an agricultural school for "training girls to become wives of farmers." Widtsoe noted that the technical schools used his books on dry farming and irrigation.[39]

They traveled from Tel Aviv east to Jerusalem. In the city they visited the Western Wall (Widtsoe used the common but inaccurate name "Wailing Wall"). They climbed up to the Temple Mount and visited the Dome of the Rock. They visited the Church of the Tomb, the Mount of Olives, Gethsemane, and other "impressive" sites.[40]

From Jerusalem, they made side trips to a number of biblical sites. They visited Jacob's Well or the Well of Sychar in Nablus, swam in the Dead Sea, and traveled to the Jordan River and the Sea of Galilee. As Widtsoe traveled, he contemplated the life of Jesus. He also considered the current state of affairs in Palestine among the various churches and sects with adherents living in the Holy Land. These hated and fought each other, in essence denying "the Prince of Peace" who advocated love for one another.[41]

Widtsoe's party also met "a handsome, bearded Arab," introduced as Sheikh Ja'coub El-Bukhari, a member of the supreme Moslem Council of Palestine and of the moderate Naqshabandi, often called the Nashāshībī faction in Palestine. El-Bukhari invited Widtsoe's party to his home, which reportedly contained a part of the house of Pilate who condemned Jesus to death. They had some refreshment

---

38. Widtsoe, *Sunlit Land*, 211.
39. Widtsoe, *Sunlit Land*, 211–12.
40. Widtsoe, *Sunlit Land*, 212.
41. Widtsoe, *Sunlit Land*, 212–13.

together. He offered them tea and coffee, which the Widtsoes declined. They explained that they could not drink the beverages because of the Word of Wisdom. Widtsoe invited El-Bukhari to dinner the following evening at the YMCA.[42]

El-Bukhari expressed deep reservations about the purchase of the homes and lands of Arabs by Jews. The purchases bothered El-Bukhari because of the condition in which the sales left the Arabs. In the future he predicted they would have no property on which to make a living, would "overeat on civilized food of meat, canned goods, white flour products, sugar and sugary products and soon lose their health and have no means of providing for their families," and become beggars.[43]

John and Leah felt a friendly attachment to El-Bukhari, and they maintained a correspondence with him for years after their 1933 visit. In one of the letters written in 1938 during the rearmament of Germany and after Italy had conquered Ethiopia, El-Bukhari expressed concern about the unsettled condition in Palestine which consisted of a British Mandate imposed by the League of Nations, Jewish immigration to Palestine, and the Arab desire for a Palestinian nation.[44]

As he visited in Palestine, Widtsoe reflected on its condition and potential future. He pointed out that in contrast with Syria, Palestine had few relative flat areas and lacked sufficient water for irrigation. He thought, unrealistically, that "Syria and Palestine should be treated as one unit," with water directed southward from Lebanon, but recognized that "for political reasons may not be possible for many years." In the intervening years, we would recognize that such a union and water diversion was impossible.[45]

John and Leah left Asia Minor by boat from Beirut on June 21, 1933. After landing in Trieste, Italy, they traveled by train by way of Milan to Calais. Crossing the English Channel, they reached London on June 29, 1933.[46]

---

42. Widtsoe, *Sunlit Land*, 213–14.

43. Widtsoe, *Sunlit Land*, 213–14.

44. Ja'coub El-Bukhari to John and Leah Widtsoe, Jan. 1, 1938, Widtsoe, *Sunlit Land*, 214–15.

45. Widtsoe, *Sunlit Land*, 215–16.

46. Widtsoe, *Sunlit Land*, 217.

Widtsoe also learned of an International Health Exposition: *"Der Mensch"* (The Man or Mankind) that was held in Dresden, Germany in 1932. German-Austrian Mission President Hyrum W. and his wife, Rose Ellen Bywater Valentine, received invitations to participate. Before they could do so, Edward P. Kimball replaced Valentine as mission president. With the Widtsoes' help, the church set up an exhibit. Widtsoe prepared the tracts for distribution. Widtsoe said it was that second most popular exhibit in the exposition. More than 1.25 million visited the LDS exhibit, and more than 250,000 picked up tracts there. More than 4,500 requested further information, which the various European missions sent them following the close of the exhibition.[47]

An Italian officer, Major Perilli, had visited the exhibit, and had corresponded with church leaders following his return to Italy. The Widtsoes met with him in Rome where they discussed the Word of Wisdom not only with the major but also with newspaper and magazine reporters. These people encouraged Widtsoe to open a mission in Italy. In 1929 Prime Minister Benito Mussolini (acting for King Victor Emanuel III) and Cardinal Secretary of State Pietro Gasparri (acting for Pope Pius XI) had signed the Lateran Concordat that established "the Catholic, Apostolic and Roman Religion is the only religion of the State" of Italy. The designation of the Catholic Church as the Italian state religion dissatisfied some of the people whom Widtsoe met.[48]

Before the Widtsoes made the trip to Rome, Widtsoe had learned that about 200 people in Italy had written to the church headquarters in Salt Lake City for information about the church. The church leadership had sent information on these inquirers to the European Mission headquarters. Widtsoe could not send missionaries to meet with them because the church had no mission in Italy at the time. The church had had a mission in Italy from 1850 when Lorenzo Snow began proselytizing there. Missionaries baptized about 180 converts, most among the Waldensians in northern Italy, before the church closed the mission in 1867. Following World War II, Italy

---

47. Widtsoe, *Sunlit Land,* 205–6; Alan K. Parrish, *John A. Widtsoe: A Biography* (Salt Lake City: Deseret Book, 2003), 426–28.

48. Widtsoe, *Sunlit Land,* 206.

functioned as a part of the Swiss Mission. In August 1966, however, the church organized a separate Italian Mission.[49]

As Widtsoe neared the end of his service as mission president in November 1933, he became particularly worried about the increasingly violent nationalism in Europe. European nations tended to have multi-party systems, and most countries were small. The Great Depression that had begun in the fall of 1929 had become increasingly onerous. Unemployment and poverty had increased. In Germany, unemployment reached 50 percent by 1933, and the government was unable to mitigate the suffering. The Nazis had become aggressively hostile in Germany, and on January 30, 1933, German president Paul von Hindenburg appointed Adolf Hitler as *Reichskanzler*. On March 23, Hitler induced the Reichstag to grant him and his cabinet extraordinary powers that permitted them to act without parliamentary approval. By law, these powers were supposed to be temporary, but Hitler simply continued to act as though the law meant nothing. Hitler's assumption of complete power awaited the death of Hindenburg on August 2, 1934, after which he assumed the offices of president and *Kanzler*.[50] By that time, Widtsoe had left Europe for the United States and Joseph F. Merrill had replaced him as European Mission president.

When Hitler came to power in Germany, Mussolini had already assumed unlimited power in Italy. From 1922 through 1925, he served as prime minister, but in 1925 he assumed the dictatorship. Victor Emmanuel III remained only as titular Italian king. Mussolini hoped to restore the grandeur of the Roman Empire and began a series of conquests in Africa in a failed attempt to do so. He assumed the *fasces*, a bundle of rods with an axe emerging from the bundle, a symbol of Roman power, as the logo of his party. To accompany the *fasces*, he adopted the name Fascist as the title of his movement. As a dictator, he ruled Italy from 1925 until his execution by Italian partisans in 1945. As Widtsoe traveled through Italy in 1932, he noted the "heavy, ugly hand [of] tyranny" that ruled

---

49. Widtsoe, *Sunlit Land*, 206; "Italy: Church Chronology," The Church of Jesus Christ of Latter-day Saints, churchofjesuschrist.org (accessed Nov. 16, 2021).

50. Ian Kershaw, *Hitler, 1889–1936: Hubris* (New York: W. W. Norton, 1998), 431, 524–26.

over Italy. Although Mussolini ruled as an oppressive dictator, he undertook an extensive project of infrastructure modernization that brought new roads, inexpensive hotels, and railroad stations to the nation. It was said that, unlike his predecessors, he made the trains run on time.[51]

Widtsoe's service as mission president brought about a number of significant changes in the church. Unfortunately, many of them were held in abeyance during World War II, which began with the German annexation of Austria and the Sudetenland in 1938. In the meantime, however, Widtsoe's reforms included dividing the European and British Mission presidencies, adopting new tracts, standardizing lessons for the auxiliaries, moving the European Mission headquarters to London, and continuing the effort to bring women and Europeans into leadership positions. All of these reforms benefitted missionary work in Europe. As he left for America in November 1933, he could be somewhat satisfied with the changes that had taken place.

---

51. Widtsoe, *Sunlit Land*, 205, 206.

CHAPTER ELEVEN

EVIDENCES AND RECONCILIATIONS

In April 1935, President Heber J. Grant, age seventy-eight, appointed Widtsoe, age sixty-three, to the co-editorship of the *Improvement Era*, the church's monthly magazine. The *Era* contained editorials; articles about church doctrine, history, and current events; instructional information for priesthood and auxiliary leaders; and poetry and stories. The magazine announced itself as the "organ of the Priesthood Quorums, Mutual Improvement Associations, and Department of Education." The masthead listed "The General Boards of the Mutual Improvement Associations" as publisher. Beginning with the June 1935 issue, the title page listed Grant and Widtsoe as editors.[1] In previous issues, Grant was listed as editor.

Modestly, Widtsoe simply said that he "was assigned to assist with the editorial work of *The Improvement Era.*" He wrote that "President Heber J. Grant was to bear the title of Editor, which has been held successively by Presidents of the Church." In fact, Widtsoe, was listed as co-editor with Grant. Harrison R. Merrill, whom Widtsoe knew well, and Elsie Talmage Brandley, daughter of recently deceased fellow Apostle James E. Talmage, served as associate editors. When Merrill returned to full-time service at BYU in 1936. Widtsoe's friend, Richard L. Evans (named an apostle in 1953), assumed the role of associate editor. With Brandley's death in August 1835, Marba Cannon Josephson became associate editor with Evans as her colleague.[2]

---

1. *The Improvement Era* 38 (June 1935): title page; Alan K. Parish, *John A. Widtsoe: A Biography* (Salt Lake City: Deseret Book Co., 2003), 325.
2. Widtsoe, *In a Sunlit Land: The Autobiography of John A. Widtsoe* (Salt Lake City: Milton R. Hunter and G. Homer Durham, 1952), 174; cf. *Improvement Era* 38 (June 1935): title page.

Arguably the most important work of long-lasting significance that Widtsoe accomplished during his service as *Improvement Era* editor was the publication of a series of articles under the titles "Evidences and Reconciliations" and "Gospel Interpretations." These essays were subsequently republished in volumes 1 and 3 of *Evidences and Reconciliations*, and a volume titled *Gospel Interpretations*, which could be considered volume 2 of *Evidences and Reconciliations*.[3]

As examples of the work Widtsoe did in *Evidences and Reconciliations*, in most of the remainder of this chapter, I summarize the contents or report on of some of the essays that Widtsoe published in volume 1. Readers will note that in his essays Widtsoe frequently used the term "man" or "men" in the generic sense of human beings, male and female, rather than meaning exclusively the male gender. At other times he simply used the term to refer to males. Also, there are occasional differences between some of the essays published in the *Improvement Era* and those republished in *Evidences and Reconciliations* (and very occasionally between printed editions of *Evidences and Reconciliations*).

Widtsoe began his discussion in volume 1 of *Evidences and Reconciliations* with a consideration of the problem of how to find truth. He quoted from the Doctrine and Covenants: "Truth is knowledge of things as they are, and as they were, and as they are to come" (93:24). He elaborated that "truth is synonymous with accurate knowledge or a product of it."

In Widtsoe's view, people obtain knowledge by learning facts through observation, which occurs in many ways. Since humans are mortal, they obtain knowledge through "imperfect senses." Because knowledge is imperfect, he wrote, humans must often "remain content ... with partial truth." Widtsoe observed that truths may also be found beyond the material universe, in "the spiritual, as well as the material worlds." For Widtsoe, though, "truth is the most precious possession of man.... Only those who seek to find the use of truth for every man's advancement, are the acceptable seekers after truth."[4]

From the search for truth, Widtsoe turned to how to gain a

---

3. Widtsoe, *Sunlit Land*, 174–75.

4. John A. Widtsoe, *Evidences and Reconciliations: Aids to Faith in a Modern Day* (Salt Lake City: Bookcraft, 1943), 3–5.

testimony of the "truth of the gospel." He defined testimony as "statements of certainty of belief." In the essay, Widtsoe outlined the path to gaining a testimony including searching for truth, recognizing one's own limitations, putting forth effort, and living a life of which a testimony is a part.[5]

Widtsoe next broached recommendations about how to know of the existence of God. He believed that those who search for knowledge of God's existence should use the same methods as in the search for any knowledge. To find evidence of God's existence, he wrote, we should employ "every power and faculty," including "observation, experimentation, feeling, prayer, and ... thought." He suggested that we know "things chiefly by their effects or by reports from others." "God, who does not reveal Himself in person to all, may be known through His works, or through His revelations to others."[6]

Widtsoe believed that one way of knowing the existence of God is through His works. Widtsoe said that "the external universe has always been to truth-loving, thinking men, an evidence of the existence of a supreme, creative directing Power." From his study and experiments as a scientist, he believed:

> Every process of nature is orderly. Chance, disorder, chaos are ruled out of the physical universe. If every condition involved in a system is precisely the same, the result, anywhere, everywhere, today or at any other time, will be the same.... The infinitely large or the infinitely small move in obedience to law.... Apparent deviations, such as the famous uncertainty principle [discovered by Werner Heisenberg] operating in the sub-atomic world, are but expressions of man's incomplete knowledge, which always disappear with increasing knowledge.[7]

As evidence for the existence of God, Widtsoe cited intelligent design and direction in the world and the universe:

> Such orderliness, such domination by law, imply intelligent planning and purpose.... Nowhere, in the age-old experience of man, has continued order been found except as the product of intelligent direction....

---

5. Widtsoe, *Evidences and Reconciliations*, 6–10.

6. Widtsoe, *Evidences and Reconciliations*, 11–12.

7. Widtsoe, *Evidences and Reconciliations*, 12–13. Heisenberg showed that an observer could not know both the position and momentum of a subatomic particle with precision. This should not be confused with the observer affect which states that by observing something, the observer affects it and may alter it.

So convincing has the accumulated knowledge of man become that sober men of science, of foremost rank, declare that to them the universe appears as a Great Thought.... There can be no planning or purpose without a mind ... The universe, itself, declares that there is intelligent purpose in nature, and that there must be, therefore, a supreme intelligence directing the universe. This is God."[8]

In elaborating on ways of gaining knowledge, Widtsoe observed that a human has other senses beyond

> seeing, hearing, tasting, smelling, and tactile feeling, ... which enable him to gather truth from the larger part of the universe beyond the reach of eye or ear.... Such, for example is the evidence of conscience. If one seeks to do right, he is warned whenever he is tempted to stray from the proper path. Similar is the evidence of prayer. The vast majority of mankind agree that prayer helps people meet or solve the problems of life. Or note the results of obedience to the law of the Lord. They who obey law find a joy not otherwise to be secured.[9]

Widtsoe believed that you could test and confirm evidence of the truths learned through the spirit just as you could those learned in the tangible world. He believed that the large number of people who believe in God and the number of those who testify of having seen him provide additional evidence of God's existence.[10]

Widtsoe admitted readily that the church did not have a monopoly on truth. He insisted, however, that it did have the true gospel of Jesus Christ.[11]

One of the most important essays in the first volume of *Evidences and Reconciliations* addressed the question: "Can Faith be Built on Theories?" He offered a resounding "No!" The principal reason for his answer is that he knew of examples of new research which resulted in new theories that superseded older ones. He cited Ptolemy who believed that the earth was the center of the solar system based on the "daily movement of the sun from east to west." He then pointed out that Nicolaus Copernicus disproved Ptolemy's

---

8. Widtsoe, *Evidences and Reconciliations*, 13–14.
9. Widtsoe, *Evidences and Reconciliations*, 14.
10. Widtsoe, *Evidences and Reconciliations*, 15–16, 20–23.
11. Widtsoe, *Evidences and Reconciliations*, 17–19.

theory when he demonstrated "that day and night result from the earth's rotation upon its axis."[12]

Widtsoe also cited the theory of a substance called "phlogiston" proposed by Georg Ernst Stahl, who argued that it was the explanation of the fire and heat that resulted from burning or rusting something. Stahl believed that things that ignite contained phlogiston, a substance that escaped from material during burning or oxidation in the form of heat and fire. French chemist Antoine Lavosier put the phlogiston theory to rest by demonstrating that "fire is but the energy released where combustible substances combine with the element oxygen."[13]

Widtsoe also pointed out that the history of the theory of evolution has undergone changes over time as scientists investigated its various aspects. He cited Darwin's view that evolution occurred because of natural selection. Widtsoe cited the phrase "'survival of the fittest'" as a synonym for natural selection. What Widtsoe did not say, however, is that the phrase "survival of the fittest" was coined by Herbert Spencer and published in his 1864 *Principles of Biology* rather than by Darwin. It is unclear that Darwin would have accepted Spencer's theory because he knew that different species and different forms of the same species survived together.[14] Darwin believed he had found an example of natural selection while he served as resident naturalist on the voyage of *HMS Beagle*. On the Galapagos Islands, he noticed the "finches ... were similar to the finches from the mainland." Each, however, "showed certain characteristics that helped them to gather food more easily in their specific habitat."[15] The two types of finches flourished in different habitats because of traits that helped them to adapt to existing conditions.

Dubious about natural selection, Widtsoe cited two books published around the time he wrote the article that argued for mutation rather than natural selection as an explanation for evolution. These books were Richard Goldschmidt's *The Material Basis of Evolution* (Yale University Press, 1940) and J. C. Willis's *The Course of*

---

12. Widtsoe, *Evidences and Reconciliations*, 24–25.

13. Widtsoe, *Evidences and Reconciliations*, 25.

14. Widtsoe, *Evidences and Reconciliations*, 25–26.

15. See "*HMS Beagle*: Darwin's Trip around the World," National Geographic, nationalgeographic.org (accessed Jan. 6, 2020).

Evolution (Macmillan, 1940). Goldschmidt argued that mutation explains evolution. Willis believed that "divergent mutation" caused evolution according to a law that scientists did not yet understand.[16] Widtsoe believed that as scientists did additional research, "future basic changes in the doctrine of evolution may well be expected."[17]

Widtsoe's views published in *Evidences and Reconciliations* were more conservative than those he had published in *Joseph Smith as Scientist* and in an *Improvement Era* article he had co-published with Edward A. Anderson. There he argued that evolution could occur as far down the scientific line as in orders, though he wrote "the limits of these orders are yet to be found."[18] In the article he also wrote with Anderson, Widtsoe suggested that "God, who is nature's master, does his work in a natural manner."[19] Clearly, Widtsoe believed that change took place in nature, and at least one time in his career he believed that change could occur through evolution as far down the chain of being as an order.

Considering Widtsoe's changing views, it is clear that by the time he wrote *Evidences and Reconciliations* he believed in evolution but was unsure about how it operated in nature, except that it occurred naturally and that God used natural means to control it. Because continuing research had potential to alter scientist's views on evolution, Widtsoe cautioned readers to "distinguish clearly between facts and the inferences from facts," another phrase for the word: theories.[20]

In various essays, Widtsoe also turned to other topics of interest. He argued that it was not wrong to doubt, but rather that "honest

---

16. Widtsoe, *Evidences and Reconciliations*, 24–27. See also the review of J. C. Willis's book by Carl L. Hubbs of the University of Michigan in *The American Naturalist* 76 (Jan.–Feb. 1942): 96, 101.

17. Widtsoe, *Evidences and Reconciliations*, 27.

18. John A. Widtsoe, *Joseph Smith as Scientist: A Contribution to Mormon Philosophy* (Salt Lake City: General Board of the YMMIA, 1908), 109–13.

19. Edward H. Anderson and John A. Widtsoe, "The Age of the Earth and the Time Length of its Creation," *Improvement Era*, 12 (Apr. 1909): 489–94. For an extended consideration of the controversy over evolution in the context of the First Presidency's statement on "The Origin of Man," including Widtsoe's views, see Thomas G. Alexander *Mormonism in Transition: A History of the Latter-day Saints, 1890–1930* (3rd ed.; Salt Lake City: Greg Kofford Books, 2012), 292–305.

20. Widtsoe, *Evidences and Reconciliations*, 27.

questioning—leads to faith" because it "impels men to inquiry which always opens the door to truth."[21]

Widtsoe followed the discussion of the need for honest questioning by insisting that higher education should not undermine faith. Responding to any who may disagree with him, Widtsoe believed that "there are those of shallow thought, again students and teachers, who declare that the teachings of the universities are in conflict with the teachings of the gospel." Instead, he wrote, "The gospel accepts and includes all truth, but it must be factual, not theoretical." Nevertheless, Widtsoe insisted that in addition to studying a subject at college, retention of faith required study of the gospel and activity in the church.[22]

Subsequent essays in the volume considered other topics he believed were important to Latter-day Saints. Widtsoe discussed liberal religion that he said consisted of such attributes as love of others and the search for truth.[23] He focused on the reasons that the Saints are a peculiar people.[24] He discussed why it required the Spirit of God to know the things of God.[25] Widtsoe compared the Urim and Thummim, which Joseph Smith used at times to translate and receive revelations, to various devices used by scientists to examine otherwise undetectable phenomena.[26]

One of the important essays in *Evidences and Reconciliations* considered various types of prophecy. Perhaps the most significant aspect of this essay is the caution Widtsoe raised about using general revelations to predict future events. He pointed out that various people have attempted to pinpoint the date of Christ's second coming by interpreting scriptures or statements by prophets to predict that or other significant events. Widtsoe cautioned forcefully against such activity, insisting, "We should not waste our valuable time and energies on remote and doubtful matters." Instead, he wrote, we should focus on learning and living the principles of the gospel.[27]

---

21. Widtsoe, *Evidences and Reconciliations*, 29.
22. Widtsoe, *Evidences and Reconciliations*, 32–35.
23. Widtsoe, *Evidences and Reconciliations*, 37–40.
24. Widtsoe, *Evidences and Reconciliations*, 41–45.
25. Widtsoe, *Evidences and Reconciliations*, 49–53.
26. Widtsoe, *Evidences and Reconciliations*, 54–57.
27. Widtsoe, *Evidences and Reconciliations*, 58–63.

In a series of essays, Widtsoe discussed various types of revelations. These included personal manifestations, continuing revelation in the LDS Church today, and special blessings to individual church members (called patriarchal blessings) intended to guide an individual's possible future life.[28]

In one essay, Widtsoe pointed out that many of the "great world religions have much in common." Many teach doctrines like the golden rule, the brotherhood of humanity, self-control and self-discipline, and humankind's immortality. He cited two theories of the reason for this similarity. One was that the concepts arose independently. Another was that they diffused from a common source. He wrote that "Latter-day Saints agree with both of these theories in part, and differ with them in part." He said that revelation from God to diverse people explained independent development. He argued, however, that diffusion seemed more likely and that it originated with the first man, Adam.[29]

Various essays considered LDS beliefs and practices. One essay pointed out LDS Church president Wilford Woodruff's 1890 Manifesto that began the end of plural marriage among orthodox Saints as a revelation.[30] Another considered angels. As Widtsoe wrote, "Angels are personages out of the spirit world, sent to earth as messengers of the Lord" for various purposes. Widtsoe added that Satan has evil angels who seek to thwart God's purposes.[31]

Widtsoe published several essays that considered aspects of the Bible. These included discussions of various translations, early books of the Bible, Noah's flood, whether the sun stood still for Joshua, and the message of the Old Testament. He pointed out that some passages or stories in the Bible may be difficult to understand. He wrote that various translations of the Bible have clarified passages that are hard to understand or that are contrary to our understanding. One example of a translation that clarifies certain concepts, he wrote, is the Smith and Goodspeed translation that clarified 1 Corinthians 15:29 on the ancient practice of baptism for the dead. Widtsoe also

---

28. Widtsoe, *Evidences and Reconciliations*, 64–77.
29. Widtsoe, *Evidences and Reconciliations*, 78–84.
30. Widtsoe, *Evidences and Reconciliations*, 85–89.
31. Widtsoe, *Evidences and Reconciliations*, 90–94.

cited some of the passages that Joseph Smith clarified in his own revision of the Bible. Widtsoe cited the King James translation that said the Lord repented in 2 Samuel 24:16, which Joseph Smith rendered as the people repented, and the Lord hardening Pharaoh's heart in Exodus 10:27, which Smith interpreted as Pharaoh hardening his heart.[32]

In trying to clarify the information about Noah's flood, Widtsoe addressed the problem of the depth of water on which Noah's ark floated. Mount Ararat where Noah's ark eventually landed was 17,000 feet high. Although the Genesis text said that water covered all the earth's mountains, it also said that the water was only fifteen cubits deep. The ancient measure of a cubit was the distance from a man's elbow to the end of his middle finger. Since the size of men's arms varied, various countries standardized the length of the cubit. Widtsoe calculated the depth of the water given in Genesis in feet using the Egyptian cubit of 20.61 inches which was the longest cubit measure. By using the Egyptian cubit, Widtsoe calculated that the Flood water was only 26 feet deep. This was far shallower than the height of Arafat and only deeper than small hills. To accept the Noah story as accurate, Widtsoe suggested that water might have descended from the heavens and run down tall mountains in streams of even less than an inch. This, he wrote, might have constituted covering them and, thus, the earth.[33]

Just as difficult as the depth of the water was the problem of the sufficiency of the earth's water supply. As he pointed out: "It is doubtful whether the water in the sky and all the oceans would suffice to cover the earth so completely." He concluded that "the fact remains that the exact nature of the flood is not known [but that] ... we set up assumptions, based upon our best knowledge, but can go no further.... The writer of Genesis made a faithful report of the facts known to him concerning the flood.... In fact, the details of the flood are not known to us."[34] In contrast with his discussion of Noah's ark, Widtsoe suggested a scientific solution to the

---

32. Widtsoe, *Evidences and Reconciliations*, 97–101.
33. Widtsoe, *Evidences and Reconciliations*, 109, 111–12.
34. Widtsoe, *Evidences and Reconciliations*, 109–10.

problems of whether the sun stood still in Gibeon as reported in Joshua 10:12–14. He wrote:

> The explanation of the occurrence made by the writer or some later copyist, implies that the earth ceased its daily rotation and annual course around the sun, to bring about the needed additional daylight for Israel's victory in battle. This may well be questioned. Even limited human knowledge suggests several simpler methods—refraction and reflection of light, for instance, by which the extension of daylight might be accomplished. Divine power may stop the rotation of the earth, let that be clearly accepted, but it certainly may have at its command other means for extending the hours of light in a day.[35]

In the essay, he did not consider the disasters throughout the earth that the sudden cessation of the earth's rotation could cause.

As a matter of caution, Widtsoe argued for a reasoned understanding of the Old Testament. He pointed out that the texts "passed through numerous hands before they reached the form available to us." Copies,

> inaccurate as well as accurate, dishonest as well as honest, unbelieving as well as believing scribes have had access to them. Material may have been added or taken away; mutilations may have occurred; through misunderstandings, or by deliberate act, errors and changes may have crept into the text.... It is probable that in some reported cases the Lord has been credited with commands that came from the lips of the human leaders of the day.... [Nevertheless] the essential message of the Lord to His children on earth has ever been preserved. The books of the Old Testament bring to us the unchanging doctrine of God's nature, eternal destiny of righteous, obedient mankind.... Without the books of the Old Testament, the earth would be poor indeed.[36]

In essaying on the attitude of the LDS Church on science, Widtsoe wrote that the church "looks with full favor upon the attempts of men to search out the facts and laws of nature." He wrote, however, that he held two reservations. They were that "the facts which are the building blocks of science must be honestly and accurately observed, [and] ... the interpretations of observed facts must be

---

35. Widtsoe, *Evidences and Reconciliations*, 113.
36. Widtsoe, *Evidences and Reconciliations*, 116–18.

distinctly labeled as inferences, and not confused with facts." On such inferences, Widtsoe cited Einstein's observation that scientists "arrange them [facts] in an orderly fashion, and then to make them understandable by 'creative thought.'"[37]

Widtsoe also returned to the relationship between the church and science in subsequent essays. In *Gospel Interpretations*, he wrote two essays on the relationship between science and religious faith.[38]

Continuing his discussion of science, Widtsoe treated topics upon which he had written previously. He wrote on the age of the earth, the means of the origin of life on earth, and evolution. In these essays, however, his discussion was much more complete, especially in his consideration of evolution.

In discussing evolution in more detail in this essay, Widtsoe seems somewhat vague in his conclusion. He stated that

> the law of evolution or change may be fully accepted." Nevertheless, "the theory of evolution [as an explanation of the development of different species] which may contain partial truth, should be looked upon as one of the changing hypotheses of science, man's explanation of a multitude of observed facts. It would be folly to make it the foundation of a life's philosophy. Latter-day Saints build upon something more secure—the operation of God's will, free and untrammeled, among the realities of the Universe."[39]

What he seems to say is that Latter-day Saints could accept evolution as an explanation of the facts discovered about the development of species as long as they also realize that the explanation might change as science makes additional discoveries and they recognize that evolution functions under the "operation of God's will."

Widtsoe returned to the question of evolution in volume 3 of *Evidences and Reconciliations*. He began the essay by arguing: "All living things, plants and animals, are subject to change.... It is an unchanging fact of nature. Living things are not static. This is the *law of evolution*." Most of the essay, however, focuses on the understanding of various scientists whom he cited on the evolution of human

37. Widtsoe, *Evidences and Reconciliations*, 125–29.

38. John A. Widtsoe, *Gospel Interpretations: Aids to Faith in a Modern Day, Being a Companion Volume to Evidences and Reconciliations* (Salt Lake City: Bookcraft, 1947), 53–57 and 58–62.

39. Widtsoe, *Evidences and Reconciliations*, 149–56.

beings. He argued that in his time scientists agreed that there was insufficient evidence to conclude that present-day human beings had descended from lower forms of life. He concluded by stressing: "Clearly the theory of evolution has added nothing to our understanding of the beginning of things. The ancient view that God is the creator of all things is still best, because it is true."[40]

In a subsequent essay, Widtsoe considered "Pre-Adamites." He agreed that sufficient evidence existed that we could not deny that such beings as Neanderthals, Cro-Magnons, and "other supposed races of manlike creatures are much the same as of many other forms of life that have lived on earth, but have long since disappeared—as for example, the dinosaurs.... The discoveries are here. They cannot be denied: but the inferences from them are subject to constant revision." He cites committed evolutionists who insist that such beings demonstrate that humans evolved from pre-Adamic beings. Again he points out, "Nevertheless, it must also be admitted that no one can safely deny that such manlike beings did at one time roam over the earth. The Lord, not man, made the earth. At his pleasure he did many things not understood by us." He considered the relationship between pre-Adamites and current human beings "speculation." "Latter-day Saints," he concluded, "are content to know that much is yet to be learned; they wait, therefore patiently, for the larger day of knowledge, without disturbing the equanimity of their lives."[41]

In other words, Widtsoe believed that we had sufficient evidence to recognize the existence of pre-Adamic beings. Nevertheless, we should accept that God created all of them, including pre-Adamites and modern human beings, but that "how all of this was accomplished is not known. The mystery of the 'creation' of Adam and Eve has not yet been revealed."[42] For some readers, this may be a more satisfactory ending to the essay than the sentence quoted in the previous paragraph.

Other essays in the series discuss such things as "The Meaning of Salvation," "The Meaning of the Atonement," and "The Difference

---

40. John A. Widtsoe, *Evidences and Reconciliations, Vol. III: Aids to Faith in a Modern Day* (Salt Lake City: Bookcraft, 1951), 135–39.

41. Widtsoe, *Evidences and Reconciliations*, 3:140–43.

42. Widtsoe, *Evidences and Reconciliations*, 3:142.

Between the Holy Spirit and the Holy Ghost." "Complete salvation, which is full and eternal life," Widtsoe wrote, "results from man's full endeavor to conform to the laws of life, the gospel of the Lord Jesus Christ."[43] In summarizing the meaning of the Atonement, Widtsoe wrote: "His [Christ's] compensation for Adam's necessary act, by which He [Christ] brought about the resurrection, is the most direct meaning of His title, Redeemer.... The 'fall' of Adam and the atonement of Jesus Christ are necessary key concepts of the gospel. Christianity stands or falls with them."[44]

In explaining the difference between the Holy Spirit and the Holy Ghost, Widtsoe wrote, "The Holy Spirit is the agent, means, or influence by which the will, power, and intelligence of God and the Godhead, personal Beings, may be transmitted throughout space.... The Holy Ghost, sometimes called the Comforter is the third member of the Godhead, and is a personage, distinct from the Holy Spirit." Since the Holy Ghost is a personage, he cannot "be everywhere present in person."[45]

A valuable essay considered whether the priesthood could "function independently of the church." The answer is yes. At various times, "the Lord has ... conferred the Priesthood on righteous men," even though it "has not existed on the earth."[46] He also wrote on the difference between holding the priesthood and possessing the keys to perform certain acts or functions. As he pointed out, a person with keys directs the performing of certain acts.[47]

Widtsoe cited Joseph Smith's statement that "a prophet is a prophet only when he was acting as such." Nevertheless, he insisted: "It would be wisdom on all occasions and with respect to all subjects in any field of human activity, to harken to the prophet's voice.... Obedience to the counsels of the prophet brings individual and collective power and joy.... Whoever quibbles about the validity of a message of the prophet would do well to engage in a serious self-examination." He wrote "In the daily lives of Latter-day Saints it is best to listen carefully to the counsel of the prophet concerning any

43. Widtsoe, *Evidences and Reconciliations*, 1:165.
44. Widtsoe, *Evidences and Reconciliations*, 1:171.
45. Widtsoe, *Evidences and Reconciliations*, 1:172–73.
46. Widtsoe, *Evidences and Reconciliations*, 1:177.
47. *Widtsoe, Evidences and Reconciliations*, 1:179–81.

subject upon which he speaks, whether technically official or unofficial."[48] He did not otherwise explain, in this essay, why he believed that members should follow the church president's advice in politics or economic policy.

Widtsoe next essayed on the question of whether the Book of Mormon Nephites had the higher priesthood before Christ's coming. He pointed out that the Book of Mormon provided no direct answer, but available evidence indicates that they did.[49]

Widtsoe turned to considering the meaning of the name Elias. He pointed out that the name had at least three meanings. In some scriptural texts, both Elias and Elijah were used for the same person at various times. A second person of the name Elias appeared to Joseph Smith to restore the dispensation of the gospel of Abraham. In a third instance, Elias can also be the name of any person commissioned to do preparatory work.[50]

Widtsoe published other essays on church doctrine. He believed that the offering of the sons of Levi in righteousness mentioned in Doctrine and Covenants 13 meant that they accepted "the gospel."[51] He wrote that man "like as Moses" (D&C 103:16) was the President of the Church and not some otherwise anonymous person who arose insisting that the passage referred to him.[52] Widtsoe cited passages from the Doctrine and Covenants and statements from Joseph Smith to substantiate the doctrine that the Quorum of the Twelve Apostles "take over the presidency of the church" on the death of the president.[53] He summarized the functions of prophets, seers, and revelators as: "A prophet is a teacher of known truth; a seer is a perceiver of hidden truth; a revelator is a bearer of new truth."[54]

In considering the question of why the church does not confine itself to spiritual matters, Widtsoe insisted that "the Church exists for the welfare of its members. It holds to the doctrine that 'men are that they might have joy.' Therefore, whatever affects human welfare,

---

48. Widtsoe, *Evidences and Reconciliations* 1:182–87.
49. Widtsoe, *Evidences and Reconciliations*, 1:188–90.
50. Widtsoe, *Evidences and Reconciliations*, 1:191–93.
51. Widtsoe, *Evidences and Reconciliations*, 1:194–95.
52. Widtsoe, *Evidences and Reconciliations*, 1:197.
53. Widtsoe, *Evidences and Reconciliations* 1:201–2.
54. Widtsoe, *Evidences and Reconciliations*, 1:201–6.

temporally or spiritually, on earth or in heaven, is accepted as the concern of the Church.'"[55]

Widtsoe addressed a number of other potentially secular subjects. He argued that it was "undesirable" to join secret oath-bound societies because the church provides a better alternative in its temples where members receive sacred ordinances and promises. These promises require members to live "the honorable life expected of faithful Latter-day Saints." He cited a long statement by Joseph Smith against joining "bands or companies, by covenant or oaths, by penalties or secrecies." In this instance, however, Smith was talking about oaths administered to those who joined the vigilante-oriented Mormon Danites in 1838 in Missouri. Widtsoe argued that oath-bound societies "are likely to take time that should be given to Church activities. Sometimes they cause loss of interest in Church duties, for no one can serve two masters with equal interest." He also believed that the church's "social and fraternal" organizations coupled with "professional and business organizations, will not only serve our needs, but will consume all the time that we can spare in these busy days." In this essay, he seems to ignore the fact that Joseph Smith, Brigham Young, and other church leaders had joined the Masons, an oath-bound organization.[56] He clarified this in volume 3 of *Evidences and Reconciliations* where he discussed the Masonic membership of Smith and other leaders.[57]

He considered also playing cards and going to movies on Sunday. He opposed the practice of playing cards with standard decks of fifty-two cards—probably because of their association with gambling—but thought playing other card games was acceptable.[58] He opposed attending movies on Sunday because, according to the scriptures, it "should be a day of rest; and it should be kept holy." Although we refrain from work if we attend the movies we would not "specialize on that day in thinking of spiritual realities, and in doing things of a spiritual nature" which would be necessary to make it holy.[59]

---

55. Widtsoe, *Evidences and Reconciliations*, 1:207–10.
56. Widtsoe, *Evidences and Reconciliations*, 1:213–14.
57. Widtsoe, *Evidences and Reconciliations*, 3:114–17.
58. Widtsoe, *Evidences and Reconciliations*, 1:215–19.
59. Widtsoe, *Evidences and Reconciliations*, 1:220–24.

He wrote an essay on the question: "Does the Payment of Tithing Cause Economic Distress?" His answer was no. He argued: "The great purpose of life is to develop such conquest over self that obedience may be willingly, easily, and gladly yielded to every commandment issuing from the mouth of the Lord." Paying tithing repays the Lord for a part of the wealth of the earth which is His anyway. Paying tithing brings blessings "even of a temporal character." He cited studies done by the church in cooperation with a government bank and USAC that, he believed, showed that payment of tithing did not cause farmers to become delinquent in paying on their loans. Apparently, however, the studies did not control for the relative wealth of those studied.[60]

Widtsoe wrote on subjects that considered marriage and family life. He urged LDS temple marriage for time and eternity. In addition, he opposed marriage between people of different faiths because he believed that "to make love secure, [husband and wife] must have much the same outlook on the major issues of life."[61]

He wrote on the place of women in the church. Although "by divine fiat" men held the priesthood, men and women were equal to each other, neither was superior. He cited Brigham Young's views that women should be educated according to their own interests in a large range of different professions. He, himself, favored home economics. Nevertheless, the place of woman was "to walk by the side of the man, not before him nor behind him."[62]

Widtsoe opposed birth control. He believed that its practice was rooted in "selfishness." If couples practiced birth control, he thought they should use the rhythm method rather than contraceptive devices or medications. In addition, he pointed out that the birth rate in advanced countries was lower than in the poorer countries, a condition that he believed militated against the improvement of society.[63]

Widtsoe wrote about good and evil, which he defined as: "Whatever conforms to the plan of God for His earth children is good; whatever is in opposition to the plan is evil." Good or evil must, he

---

60. Widtsoe, *Evidences and Reconciliations*, 1:225–28.
61. Widtsoe, *Evidences and Reconciliations*, 1:237–40.
62. Widtsoe, *Evidences and Reconciliations*, 1:241–45.
63. Widtsoe, *Evidences and Reconciliations*, 1:246–51.

argued, result from the actions of human beings. God allows Satan and his followers to tempt us with evil on Earth to give humans the opportunity to exercise their free agency to choose good or evil.[64]

Following a discussion of evil, Widtsoe wrote on whether there is a personal devil. His answer was yes, and he explained that the Lucifer, one of the leaders in the preexistence, chose to oppose God's plan for the salvation of humankind. After God banished Lucifer from his presence, Lucifer—now Satan—and his spirit followers took to the earth as adversaries and tempters to thwart God's plan by convincing humans to reject his plan for salvation and choose evil instead. Speaking to his prophets, God has explained that we can resist Satan's enticements. If we choose to resist, Satan has no power to force us to adopt evil ways.[65]

Widtsoe moved from a discussion of Satan to a consideration of the adversary's most devoted followers, the so-called Sons of Perdition. Widtsoe argues: "It is probable that only personages who have acquired similar full knowledge [as Lucifer did] who willfully and deliberately deny the truth, when they know it to be the truth, and commit the unpardonable sin ... [can] become sons of perdition." An infinitesimally small few have knowledge enough to become Sons of Perdition.[66]

Continuing the discussion of evil, Widtsoe raised the question of why the Lord permits war. Using free agency, humans engage in war just as they do other things that break God's commandments.

> The Lord abhors war or contention, whether in the household, office, or on the fields of battle.... [Nevertheless] He may, [at times] in His great mercy, ameliorate the terrors of warfare and turn the tide of battle in behalf of the righteous.... However, when human rights and freedom, the plan of salvation itself, are the issues, the raging battle becomes the battle of the Lord, and those who have truth, and fight for it, should plead with the Lord for help, and in the course of time will receive it, for it has been said: "The Lord shall fight for you" (Exodus 14:14).[67]

---

64. Widtsoe, *Evidences and Reconciliations*, 1:255–63. The LDS Church today prefers the term "moral agency" to "free agency."

65. Widtsoe, *Evidences and Reconciliations*, 1:258–63.

66. Widtsoe, *Evidences and Reconciliations*, 1:264–66.

67. Widtsoe, *Evidences and Reconciliations*, 1:267–70.

Widtsoe considered whether a soldier should love his enemy. The essay includes a long discussion of the need to oppose sin and not show it "love or mercy" and to measure "all human affairs … by the standards of right." Nevertheless, Widtsoe wrote, "the soldier can and should love his enemy, but not in the sense that he forgets the greater love of the cause [the plan of salvation of Jesus Christ] by which in the end the enemy and all others will be blessed."[68]

In considering the Celestial Kingdom, Widtsoe questioned whether all who reach the highest degree of heaven in the afterlife will become exalted. He compared it to a college graduation in which all receive a diploma, but some graduate with honors, some with high honors, and some with highest honors. Quoting Joseph Smith, Widtsoe said, "'In the celestial glory there are three heavens or degrees.' Full exaltation means the attainment of the highest of these three degrees in celestial glory." Fulfilling certain requirements is necessary in LDS theology to achieve this highest degree. One of these requirements is marriage in the temple which is sealed by the Holy Spirit of promise. This may be done either in person or vicariously for the dead.[69]

In general, Widtsoe wrote that little children who die before the age of accountability are redeemed though Christ. In a strange part of the essay, however, Widtsoe qualified his statement by writing, "If in their pre-existent state they have not made themselves unworthy." He does not explain what would make anyone who agreed to accept God's plan and who did not follow Lucifer unworthy when born on earth.[70] Perhaps Widtsoe's assertion was influenced by other statements, since discredited and repudiated, that some people, especially Blacks, were somehow "less valiant" in the pre-earth life.

Following the essay on little children, Widtsoe wrote on the question of whether people who lived on Earth before Jesus Christ will be resurrected before those who came after. Widtsoe argued that the resurrection will be orderly. Quoting Alma 40:19, Widtsoe said that those who died before Christ's resurrection will come forth first. Moreover, they will come forth in order of their faithfulness.[71]

---

68. Widtsoe, *Evidences and Reconciliations*, 1:271–74.
69. Widtsoe, *Evidences and Reconciliations*, 1:277–78.
70. Widtsoe, *Evidences and Reconciliations*, 1:279.
71. Widtsoe, *Evidences and Reconciliations*, 1:280–81.

Widtsoe then raised the question in another essay of whether it is "Possible to Progress from One Glory to Another [in Heaven]?" Widtsoe believed that deceased people could move within each of the three degrees, or kingdoms, of heavenly glory, but not from one kingdom to a higher one. Widtsoe apparently disagreed with Brigham Young and some others who believed that people could advance from a lower kingdom to a higher kingdom.[72]

In his essay on the so-called Adam-God theory, he makes clear that the church does not accept the teaching that Adam was God the Father. He went further to deny that Brigham Young had preached the theory.[73] In this he was mistaken. Young did preach the doctrine.[74]

After a lengthy essay on Adam-God, Widtsoe discussed the question of where the lost tribes of Israel are now. He pointed out that after Solomon's reign the Israelites divided into two kingdoms: Israel in the north in Samaria and Judah in the south. During the reign of King Hoshea in the northern kingdom of Israel, the Assyrians invaded Israel, deported part of the ten tribes, and resettled them in northern Mesopotamia and in Media.[75]

Historical evidence shows that some of the Israelites escaped from Assyrian rule and traveled northward. We do not know just where they went, but scriptures locate them in the north and Jeremiah speaks of them returning "out of the north country." 2 Esdras 13:40–47 in the Apocrypha says they settled in the "region ... called Arsareth." Book of Mormon prophet Ether prophesied that they will be gathered "from the four quarters of the earth, and from the north countries." In the Saints' Kirtland, Ohio, temple, Moses appeared and committed the keys "of ... the leading of the ten tribes from the land of the north" to Joseph Smith and Oliver Cowdery (D&C 110:11). Widtsoe also cited the view frequently held in the nineteenth and twentieth centuries that the Israelites were disbursed

---

72. Widtsoe, *Evidences and Reconciliations*, 1:282–83; Thomas G. Alexander, *Brigham Young and the Expansion of the Mormon Faith*, Volume 31 in the Oklahoma Western Biographies Series, ed. Richard W. Etulain (Norman: University of Oklahoma Press, 2019), 209–10.

73. Widtsoe, *Evidences and Reconciliations*, 1:287–90.

74. Alexander, *Brigham Young and the Expansion*, 215–19, 226.

75. Widtsoe, *Evidences and Reconciliations*, 1:291–92.

throughout northern Europe and that their presence in that region explained the success of LDS missionaries in converting and gathering large numbers of people in the area at that time. Nevertheless, some have argued, as Widtsoe noted, that Israelites were so widely scattered that "the blood of Israel is now found in almost every land and among every people."[76]

In concluding this discussion, Widtsoe pointed out that wherever the lost tribes are located, LDS doctrine holds that "it is part of the mission of the Church to gather Israel into the fold of the truth," that is, into the church. For that reason, the church has committed enormous amounts of time and money to preach the gospel throughout the earth to "bring all men into the house of Israel." As a caution, he argued that "the location of the lost tribes, [is] of itself unimportant," and that people waste time in trying to determine just where they are and ignore more important matters.[77]

Widtsoe turned to the question of the extent of knowledge that Latter-day Saints had about the American West when they emigrated from Nauvoo, Illinois. He pointed out that Joseph Smith had prophesied that the Saints would settle in the "midst of the Rocky Mountains." After a lengthy essay about the knowledge they had of the West, Widtsoe concludes that "the choosing of the Great Basin for settlement, and the locating of their chief city in the Great Salt Lake Valley were products of the spirit of prophecy and revelation."[78] We should understand that Widtsoe apparently did not have the minutes of the semi-secret Council of Fifty available when he wrote the essay. These clearly reveal that the Saints had already decided to settle in the area of the Great Salt Lake before they left Nauvoo.

Widtsoe wrote on the question whether systems like communism, fascism, nazism, socialism, and related systems are the same as the now-abandoned LDS economic system, the United Order. His answer was an emphatic "No!"[79]

After rejecting various theories about the reason for practicing plural marriage, Widtsoe asserted that "the only acceptable explanation,

---

76. Widtsoe, *Evidences and Reconciliations*, 1:293–94.
77. Widtsoe, *Evidences and Reconciliations*, 1:194–95.
78. Widtsoe, *Evidences and Reconciliations*, 1:296–300.
79. Widtsoe, *Evidences and Reconciliations*, 1:301–5.

is that the principle of plural marriage came as a revelation from the Lord to the Prophet Joseph Smith for the Church." He rejected assertions that there was a surplus of women, that women preferred to marry more refined men, or that Mormon polygamy was born of lust. He also insisted that women in plural marriage were invariably treated equally, something that subsequent research has shown was not always true. Widtsoe also cited the inaccurate statistic that "plural marriage was practiced by between two and four percent of the Church membership from 1843 to 1890." More recent research has shown that at various times at least a quarter of all LDS families were polygamous. Nevertheless, Widtsoe pointed out that we do not know why the Lord instituted it at the time.[80]

Widtsoe ended the first volume of *Evidences and Reconciliations* with essays on the importance of family prayer and who should partake of the sacrament. His answers are similar to those generally preached now in the LDS Church. Prayer, he said, is "the beginning of wisdom," and is significant as a means of communing between God and humankind. Members should partake of the sacrament worthily, it was instituted by Christ at the last supper, and the Lord allowed members to use water rather than wine in the sacrament because the type of drink is not as important as the renewal of members' baptismal covenants.[81]

In *Gospel Interpretations*, published in 1947, Widtsoe wrote five essays on the Word of Wisdom. In them he cited scientific evidence to propose prohibitions that went far beyond the actual wording and usual interpretation of Doctrine and Covenants 89. He urged members to avoid all substances containing caffeine and advised against chocolate.[82] Three years later, he collaborated with his wife in publishing *The Word of Wisdom: A Modern Interpretation* that incorporated the information from his *Gospel Interpretations* essays plus a great deal more.[83] As a result of these writings, some humorists in the church began referring to the Widtsoe's interpretation of the Word of Wisdom as the Word of Widtsoe. In the third volume of

---

80. Widtsoe, *Evidences and Reconciliations*, 1:306–10.

81. Widtsoe, *Evidences and Reconciliations*, 1:311–20.

82. Widtsoe, *Gospel Interpretations*, 175–194.

83. John A. Widtsoe and Leah D. Widtsoe, *The Word of Wisdom: A Modern Interpretation* (Salt Lake City: Deseret Book Co., 1950).

Evidences and Reconciliations, Widtsoe wrote an additional essay on the Word of Wisdom. Though less lengthy than either the previous essay or the book he wrote with his wife, this essay still cautioned against eating chocolate or drinking anything containing caffeine as well as advised against eating large quantities of meat, which Section 89 also advised.[84]

In addition to the works mentioned above, Widtsoe wrote a number of other essays and books to help members and others interested in knowing about the church. Among the most important were *Priesthood and Church Government* (1939), which explained how the church operated and *Program of the Church of Jesus Christ of Latter-day Saints* (2nd ed., 1937), which included additional readings by J. Wiley Sessions and Merrill D. Clayson. He wrote the latter book to supplement his teaching at the University of Southern California. He also wrote to defend the Book of Mormon in *Seven Claims of the Book of Mormon: A Collection of Evidences* (1937) with Franklin S. Harris Jr.

Widtsoe wrote a large number of essays and books to explain his views of gospel principles and other topics to church members. After publishing the first volume of *Evidences and Reconciliations,* Widtsoe collected subsequent essays in *Gospel Interpretations* and Volume 3 of *Evidences and Reconciliations.* These latter two explored in great detail some of the essays in the first volume as well as treated additional topics. During his lifetime, church members recognized Widtsoe as both a member of the Quorum of the Twelve Apostles and as a famous scientist and intellectual who published essays on church topics that many accepted as authoritative.

---

84. Widtsoe, *Evidences and Reconciliations,* 3:154–57.

CHAPTER TWELVE

FAMILY AND ANALYSIS

In 1893 while Widtsoe was studying at Harvard, he began to take an interest in Leah Dunford, one of a group of young women who came to Harvard to take a summer school course that University of Utah Professor Maude May Babcock taught. Somewhat reluctantly, Widtsoe and some of his LDS friends took the women sightseeing. After he met her, the two spent some time with one another. John was clearly interested in Leah, and the two saw a great deal of one another during the summer. They took long walks together, shared romantic evenings in Longfellow Park, and met for lunch between classes.[1]

Although impressed with Leah, Widtsoe had reservations about pursuing a relationship. He had already amassed considerable debt while earning his bachelor's and master's degrees, which he believed would take two or three years to repay. He understood, also, that he would increase his debt and that he would have to go Europe to study for the four years for a PhD in chemistry.[2]

In spite if these reservations, between 1893 and 1897 the young couple corresponded, but because of the distance between Utah and Massachusetts, they met only infrequently. In spite of potential future hardships of debt and travel, John and Leah were in love, and in the fall of 1897, they agreed to marry on June 1, 1898, the birthday of Brigham Young, Leah's maternal grandfather. On June 1, Joseph F. Smith, then a counselor in the First Presidency, sealed them for time and eternity in the Salt Lake Temple. Leah's father,

---

1. John A. Widtsoe, *In a Sunlit Land: The Autobiography of John A. Widtsoe* (Salt Lake City: Milton R. Hunter and G. Homer Durham, 1952), 228–30.
2. Widtsoe, *Sunlit Land*, 231–32.

Dr. Alma B. Dunford, DDS, honored them with a dinner at his home in Salt Lake City. Leah's mother, Susa Young Gates (who was divorced from Dunford), sponsored a reception and dance for them at College Hall on the Brigham Young Academy campus. Leah was twenty-four, John was twenty-six.[3]

When they married, Leah was arguably a better-known public figure than John. A member of one of Utah's first families and daughter of one of Utah's foremost women, she had also taught home economics at Brigham Young Academy, engaged frequently in public speaking, published articles in magazines and newspapers, and performed musically.[4]

The couple agreed to rear a large family and were saddened when only three of their seven children survived to adulthood and one son died as a young man. Two sons: John Jr. and Mark, and two daughters: Helen and Mary died prematurely. Three others lived: Anna (b. 1899), Karl Marsel (called Marsel, b. 1902), and Leah Eudora (b. 1912). Marsel taught seminary for the LDS Church in Preston, Idaho, and planned to matriculate at Harvard to study business administration. To the deep sorrow of his parents, sisters, and friends, Marsel died of pneumonia in 1927 at age twenty-four. Anna served an LDS proselytizing mission in the southern United States, took a degree in library science, married Lewis J. Wallace, and bore three children: John, Joanne, and Margaret. Anna and Lewis later divorced. Leah Eudora (whom the Widtsoes' called Eudora, after Leah's mother's sister) studied in Europe, graduated from the University of Utah, and married G. Homer Durham, an educator, university president, and later member of the church's First Quorum of the Seventy. They raised three children: Carolyn, Leah Eudora, and George Homer II.[5]

John Widtsoe considered Leah's and his family life "ideal." As one might expect in the late nineteenth and early twentieth centuries, "Leah took the burden of the house." His roles as PhD student, chemist, administrator, college and university president, apostle, educator, and mission president occupied virtually all his time. In spite

---

3. Widtsoe, *Sunlit Land*, 232–33.
4. Widtsoe, *Sunlit Land*, 233–34.
5. Widtsoe, *Sunlit Land*, 237–38.

of the "burden" of housework, Leah served as an LDS temple worker, presided over the Salt Lake Federation of Women's Clubs, and was on the board of the Salt Lake Council of Women.[6] She helped to found and served as president of the Salt Lake City Federation of Women Voters. She worked actively in the Salt Lake Council of Women, the National League of Pen Women and the Women's Legislative Council. In 1923 she represented Utah at the National Home Economics Movement Conference. She accompanied John during his visits with farmers while he directed the experiment station. During those visits, she drew on her home economics education to discuss with farm women such things as foods, housecleaning, and health. She lobbied successfully with Reed Smoot for legislation to provide the states with funds for research in home economics.

Both Widtsoes were fortunate to have fallen in love and married wisely. As a woman who fashioned a distinguished career of her own, Leah complimented John's career and activities. John was one of the first three members of the Quorum of the Twelve Apostles to hold a PhD in science. The others were James E. Talmage and Joseph F. Merrill. As scientists, the three enriched the church leadership by offering perspectives in the church's highest quorums, in their speeches and writings, and as they traveled throughout the church in fields other than scripture study and business.

Had Widtsoe never served as an apostle, however, his contributions and accomplishments would likely have been both noteworthy and unusual. His decision to specialize in biochemistry led him to earn the PhD at Göttingen under Bernhard Tollens, the world's premier authority in the field. He advanced the field of biochemistry through his research on the chemistry of plants and by writing books on irrigation and dry farming. Significantly, his research and writing garnered international acclaim and more importantly influenced agricultural practice in the United States and throughout the world. Picking himself up after William J. Kerr fired him as director of the USAC Experiment Station, he organized the agricultural science department at BYU. A few years later, he replaced Kerr as president of USAC. In that position, he revitalized the experiment station, but

6. Widtsoe, *Sunlit Land*, 237–38.

more significantly he induced the legislature to restore the appropriations that Kerr had lost because he had attempted to challenge the University of Utah by expanding USAC course offerings beyond agricultural topics. Instead of challenging University of Utah president Joseph T. Kingsbury and Dean Joseph F. Merrill, as Kerr had done, Widtsoe worked with them to secure approval to offer agricultural engineering at USAC.

Widtsoe has been the only person to serve as president of both USAC and the University of Utah. His appointment as U of U president occurred under circumstances similar to his appointment to the Logan institution. Like Kerr, Kingsbury had lost the confidence of a substantial portion of the faculty and board of trustees. While Kingsbury served as president, Joseph Merrill, then a dean at the U, had worked diligently, but with little success, to obtain a clear definition of the faculty's administrative authority. With the support of the board, however, Kingsbury had insisted on unilateral rule. A controversy over the political views and activities of students and faculty led Kingsbury to fire or demote several faculty members. Kingsbury's actions led to a number of faculty resignations and an investigation by the American Association of University Professors. The AAUP report criticized both Kingsbury and the board of trustees for failing to determine the cause and correctness of faculty actions and views. Under considerable pressure, Kingsbury resigned as president.

Unfortunately, the U of U board's executive committee, under the leadership of Richard Young, acted without consulting the other board members when they decided to appoint Widtsoe to replace Kingsbury. Some board members and some in the public charged LDS interference in Widtsoe's appointment. When the board members listened to Widtsoe explain his views of university administration, however, his obvious competence, his plans for faculty governance, and his sincere demeanor convinced even those board members who had opposed his appointment that he would serve as excellent university president.

At first, Widtsoe was reluctant to accept the appointment. He had reservations because he had enjoyed success in Logan. Moreover, the president of the University of Utah had a smaller salary than his at USAC. He consulted church leaders, most of whom recommended that he accept the presidency. After deliberation, he took the position because of his commitment to public service.

Significantly, Widtsoe won the approval of both the faculty and the board. He immediately instituted a university constitution with a significant degree of faculty governance based on a similar document that the University of Illinois had recently adopted. This action together with a successful effort to endear himself to the faculty, the board, and the public made his tenure a notable success.

He retained the position of president of the U until 1921 when the First Presidency called him to the apostleship. He took an even bigger cut in salary when accepting that position because as an apostle he earned only a third as much as he had earned as U of U president. He and Leah had recently purchased a home near the University of Utah campus, and he realized that the greatly reduced salary would result in significant pressure on their standard of living. Nevertheless, he accepted the call because of his faith and his commitment to the church, its programs, and its teachings.

During the early years of his apostleship, Widtsoe worked with foreign governments and with Utah senator Reed Smoot (also an apostle) to reopen European countries to the church's missionaries. During World War I, most governments prohibited foreign missionaries from entering. Although Widtsoe and Smoot hit a number of roadblocks as they sought permission for American missionaries to enter, they were finally able to gain the missionaries readmission to most European countries.

In 1927 the First Presidency called Widtsoe to return to Europe as European Mission president. Leah and their youngest daughter, Eudora, accompanied him to Liverpool. Some of Widtsoe's major accomplishments as mission president include the reform and reorganization of several mission functions. Previously, the European Mission president had served concurrently as president of the British Mission. Because of the time constraints caused by presiding in two offices, Widtsoe recommended and the First Presidency and Twelve agreed to separate the two presidencies, and the church established the British Mission headquarters in London. As a matter of convenience, Widtsoe moved the European Mission headquarters from Liverpool to London as well. In an effort to maintain better relationships with the mission presidents over whom he presided, Widtsoe inaugurated annual conferences of the presidents of European missions. Widtsoe supervised the opening of a mission in the Czech Republic. Recognizing the need to replace tracts that the church had used in Europe for decades, Widtsoe wrote new tracts himself, and he revised and adopted others already in use in the United States. To the extent could, Widtsoe called Europeans to serve in branch and district positions. Previously, American missionaries held most of these positions.

In 1932, LDS president Heber Grant asked Widtsoe to travel to Palestine and Syria to dedicate the grave of Joseph W. Booth who had died while serving as Turkish Mission president. John and Leah traveled to the Near East where he accomplished this task in addition to installing a new mission president of the Palestine-Syria Mission. While in Palestine, he also met with Sheikh Ja'coub El-Bukhari, a member of the Moslem council with whom he discussed farming and other activities.

While serving as mission president, Widtsoe witnessed the changes that Fascism and Nazism made in Italy and Germany. He did not favor the abolition of democracy caused by these changes, but he could do nothing to reverse them.

Widtsoe and Leah took a particular interest in the Word of Wisdom. Drawing on his scientific education and Leah's training in home economics, the two wrote a book in which they reinterpreted the principles revealed and published in Doctrine and Covenants 89. Their views went beyond those preached as official doctrine by the church, including avoiding all caffeinated drinks and chocolate. Their views may have been scientifically sound, but they did not comport with some of the words in Section 89.

In addition to reopening Europe to American missionaries and the changes Widtsoe made in the administration of missionary work in Europe, arguably his most important contribution to the church consisted of a series of articles he wrote while co-editor of the *Improvement Era*. He called them *Evidences and Reconciliations*, and they were subsequently published in three volumes that provided a thoughtful perspective on church doctrine and practice and on scientific principles. Widtsoe's son-in-law, G. Homer Durham, later edited and combined the three volumes into a single book.[7]

Widtsoe's most important contributions in *Evidences and Reconciliations* were his recognition of evolution as a significant scientific contribution. He wrote, "All living things, plants and animals, are subject to change. Every observer of nature, certainly all plant and animal breeders, know this to be true. It is an unchanging fact of nature. Living things are not static. This is the *law* of evolution."[8] By the time he wrote about evolution in *Evidences and Reconciliations*, however, he rejected the theory of natural selection as a means of explaining the origin and development of the human species. He concluded: "The ancient view that God is the creator of all things is still the best, because it is true."[9]

By the time of his death in 1952, Widstoe had become one of the LDS Church's best-known theologians and intellectuals. The scientific, educational, and religious communities would have been much poorer without his contributions.

7. John A. Widtsoe, *Evidences and Reconciliations, Volumes 1-2-3*, arranged by G. Homer Durham (Salt Lake City: Bookcraft, 1960).

8. John A. Widtsoe, *Evidences and Reconciliations, Vol. III* (Salt Lake City: Bookcraft, 1951), 135.

9. Widtsoe, *Evidences and Reconciliations*, 3:139.

INDEX

Note: In the entries for subjects found in *Evidences and Reconciliations* and *Gospel Interpretations* readers should also consult the Widtsoe, John Andreas as well. Some will be found there rather than in the other entries.

Sub-entries are reported in numerical order as they appear in the text rather than alphabetically.

Council, 159; National Home Eco-
nomics Movement Conference, 159
Widtsoe, Mark, 158
Widtsoe, Osborne (Asbjorn) Johannes
Peder, vii, 4, 5, 75–76
William Budge Memorial Hospital, 90
Willis, J. C., *The Course of Evolution*,
139–40
Wisconsin, S. S., 6
Wise, George C., 75, 76
Whitmore, George C., 79
Woodury, Nettie, 125
Woodruff Manifesto, 32
Word of Wisdom, 83, 126, 127, 162
*Word of Wisdom: A Modern Interpreta-
tion, The*, 155
Work, Hubert, 108
World War I, viii, 84, 117, 126, 161
World War II, 125, 126, 132–33
Wyoming, 102, 104, 105
Wyoming v. *Colorado*, 104–5; federal
government creates danger for
Green-Colorado River States in,
104–5

Y

Yahveh, 130
Young, Brigham, 106, 128, 157; char-
ters educational institutions, 8, 43;
Brigham Young's Discourses (JAW ed-
ited), 86; and Masons, 149; education
of women, 150; progression from one
degree of glory to another, 153
Young Men's Mutual Improvement
Association, 7, 48, 63, 86
Young Women's Mutual Improvement
Association, 48
Young, Richard W., 73, 74

Z

Zürich, Switzerland, vii, 30–31